DOWN FROM THE LONELY MOUNTAIN

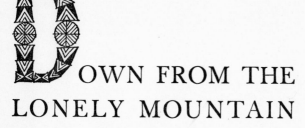

Down from the Lonely Mountain

California Indian Tales

RETOLD BY JANE LOUISE CURRY

Illustrated by Enrico Arno

HARCOURT, BRACE & WORLD, INC., NEW YORK

To Michael and Mark,
Cindy, Jennie and Sally,
Miles and Bobbie and Jamie,
Betsy, Sara, Sharon and Ann,
and especially Miriam Moore and the Guides

CONTENTS

7

The Beginning of the World and the Making of California

FAR to the south, in the seasons before there was this world where animal folk and Indians dwell, there was a Lonely Mountain. It was the only land under the arches of the sky. Everything else was water. To the north, to the south, to the east and west, there was nothing but the smooth wetness of deep water.

There were animals there, for though the mountain's sides were steep, there were ledges and gullies where they had crept for shelter when the water had first swept the earth away. Manzanita apples and buckthorn berries and pine nuts had been their food at first. When these were gone, they ate leaves and twigs and pine needles; and when these in turn had been devoured, the animals ate stems, trunks, and roots.

The mountain was thus made bare, and the water was empty of fish. There was nothing to eat but the earth of the mountain itself; and so hungry were the animals that they were driven to eat even that. Many creatures died. Eagle was their chieftain, and it pained him sorely to think that soon they all must die. Coyote was second in command, and it pained him sorely to see that the mountain was shrinking daily as the animals ate of it and that soon it would dwindle to nothing. He feared the water.

One day Coyote said to Eagle, his chief, "Is there no way in which we can obtain more earth? Can we not somehow make more mountains?"

Eagle sighed heavily, shifting on his perch of rock. "If there is, I do not know of it," he said.

Coyote paced about in a circle. "There must be a way," he muttered. "There must be a way. Surely someone knows. Who would know? Magpie is the oldest. I shall go and fetch Magpie."

Coyote trotted downhill to the rock where Magpie dozed. "Hai, Old Bird!" he cried. "Come with me to Eagle's perch. There is a question we would put to you." So Magpie came.

Chief Eagle greeted graciously the ancient bird and then asked of him, "Is there any way that we may obtain earth? We are running out of mountain. Can we not make more?"

And Magpie said, "Yes."

"Yes? Yes!" chorused Eagle and Coyote. "Where? Tell us from where we may fetch it, Ancient Feathered One."

"From down below," said Magpie, stretching his wing to point at the lapping waters. "Good earth, not stones and powdered rock like this our mountain."

The animals were overjoyed at the spreading news and gathered in a crowd at the water's edge to see whom Eagle would send for the earth and to watch. All of the waterfowl were called to the fore of the gathering so that Eagle might explain the task that lay before them. "The earth lies at the bottom of the waters," he said, "and so it is to you, the divers, that we turn for help. You are our only hope."

The first duck to volunteer was a handsome green-headed fellow who borrowed a tule basket from his wife and dived in straightaway. It was but a few moments before he floated up again, half dead from exhaustion, still clutching the basket. "There is no bottom," he gasped weakly as they drew him to shore at Eagle's feet.

"There must be!" cried Coyote. "It was the basket! The basket slowed him down." And Eagle agreed.

To the next duck he said, "Take no basket, but when you reach the ground at the bottom, take hold of it, bite off a piece, and fill your ears and beak with it." All thought that this was a good plan.

Duck after duck tried to reach the earth at the bottom of the waters, and duck after duck came floating to the top of the waters, some stunned with the weight of the water and some near death. One flew so high to gather speed for a plummeting dive that he hit the water with a splash that knocked him senseless. Of the strongest swimmers, some were gone beneath the waters for half a day; but in the end they floated up to lie on the water until friends could tow them ashore. Six long days they dived and found no bottom.

At last there was no one left to go except Mudhen. Coyote in his fear was angry at the others for their failure, for Mudhen was certainly too puny to succeed where the sleek and sure had failed. But Eagle said kindly to Mudhen, "Now you must go. It must be that you are meant to find the earth."

Mudhen swam out from the shore and disappeared beneath the water. For hours the animals kept vigil. Night crept over them and after it the pale gray light of dawn. There was no sign at all of Mudhen until the first ray of the morning sun touched on the waters. At that moment Mudhen floated up and lay motionless upon the water, dead. As she was brought ashore, all of the animal folk wailed their grief, for not only was a good friend lost, but it seemed that their last hope had died with her. Coyote's howl was loudest. Eagle, however, remained calm, turning Mudhen gently over so that he could see claws, beak, and ears. The earth was there. Mudhen *had* reached the bottom.

Eagle cried, "My people, here is the earth!" and he held a bit of it aloft until the wailing died away. Then he sent Earthworm to search under all of the rocks for chiyu and telis and pele seeds. Earthworm came back with very few, for the starving animals had scoured the ground quite thoroughly, but those few he gave to Eagle. With great care Eagle ground up the seeds, mixed them with the precious black earth, and added water. Even as he began to stir the mixture, it started to swell, spreading along the rocks and into the water.

It grew and grew and spread and thickened. Coyote, curious, touched the closest edge and found that it felt much like the dough of uncooked bean cakes. The mark of his paw remained on the earth and grew larger with it as it spread out to the north, pushing back the water. By the next day no water could be seen except a wide strip across the western horizon. By the third day even that was but a thin ribbon at the edge of the western sky. On the sixth day the earth seemed no longer to move, and Eagle announced that it had stopped growing.

"We must see if the earth is ready for us," said Eagle, and then he turned to Wolf. "You must go around the earth to make sure that it has stopped growing and that none of it is breaking off at the edges."

Wolf trotted off to the north, making his way where the Sierra Nevada now is, and around to the west. The earth stretched so far that he grew more and more excited and ran even more swiftly back down the western rim of the land, where the Coast Range now lies. When finally he returned to the Lonely Mountain, he reported back to Eagle, saying, "The land is wide and well fastened at the edges and only waits for us to fill it."

But Eagle shook his head. "Did you not look behind you as you went, friend Wolf? If not, look now. Your flying feet kicked up the wet spongy earth, leaving great ridges where you passed!"

And it was so. Puffy ridges arose and faded away into the northern distance, marking Wolf's returning path. Far inland, smaller humps and ridges marked his outward journey. But as Eagle and his people watched, the wet earth settled a bit, and hillocks and ridges appeared to smooth themselves. "The earth is too wet for us to use," declared Eagle. "We must wait until it dries. None must touch it until six more days have passed."

And the animals agreed that it should be so. "Very well," they said. "We shall wait until it has dried."

For Coyote six days seemed six ages. He itched to see how far the new earth stretched and to choose for himself the best place in all the land to build a lodge. If he could only scout the land out before the sixth day, he could find the richest earth and the best view! "I don't see why I shouldn't," he told himself. "After all, it looks quite solid now." Thus it was that very early on the third day, before the birds had awakened, he slipped from his ledge on the mountainside and jogged off to the north, going the same way that Wolf had gone. As he traveled along where the Sierras now tower, the soft earth cracked and split, and what had been rounded ridges became broken and rough, much as they are today. When at last Coyote thought to look behind himself, the sight of the jagged mountains frightened him. "What will Eagle say?" he wondered. "What will the animals think?"

Hoping to get back before he was missed, Coyote turned west, treading carefully, and headed back down the high mounds of the western coast. Yet no matter how softly he stepped, the earth cracked and wrinkled, and that is why there are mountains there as well. Halfway back to the Lonely Mountain, he tiptoed so close to the edge of the still soft land that his right forepaw slipped and gouged out what is now San Francisco Bay. Ashamed of the damage his greed had caused, he crept home and hid where none could see him.

On the fifth day Eagle summoned Prairie Falcon and Khotoi the Raven. To them he said, "You must fly around the world to see whether it is hardened yet. But take care that you do not touch it. Already there are too few smooth places left."

Prairie Falcon and Khotoi were delighted to be chosen as scouts, for with the sixth day so very close upon them, all of the animals were consumed with curiosity about the land that was to be their home. Prairie Falcon soared northward high above the Sierra Nevada, and Khotoi headed up the Coast Range; then both headed south again the way they had come, each eager to be first with the news. Upon their return Eagle asked, "How fares the earth? Tell us whether it is yet hardened."

"Not yet, but almost," cried Prairie Falcon and Khotoi. "And the land is beautiful! The valleys are rich, and the mountains are almost as high as the sky."

"Fly up and back again," said Eagle, "and this time you must flap your wings as hard as you can, for that will help to dry out the earth." And they did so, Prairie Falcon soaring up the Sierra Nevada with a slow but strong beating of wings, and Khotoi fluttering and flapping up the Coast Range, keeping as low above the mountaintops as he dared. When at last the earth seemed dry and the rushing of their wings raised clouds of dust, both returned to the mountain in the south.

"How fares the earth?" asked Eagle. "Is it hardened yet?"

"Yes!" they cried, and Prairie Falcon turned to point proudly. "See," he said. "See how strong my mountains are. They reach highest to the sky."

"They do not!" objected Khotoi. "Mine in the west are higher. Ask Wolf. Ask Coyote if it is not so!"

Prairie Falcon laughed and pointed again with his wing. "You have but to look! See, you flapped so hard and flew so low over the damp ridges that you mashed them down!" It was so. All of the animals looked out across the land and saw that the mountains along the coast *had* shrunk and that now the jagged Sierra Nevada were the higher.

"Take heart," said Eagle to the disappointed Khotoi. "It shows that your wings are strong, and it looks quite good. Much better than before, in fact."

With that, Eagle decided that Coyote should be forgiven for making the rough mountain ridges, and he

called him out of his hiding place. Once back at Eagle's side, Coyote swelled up with the success of his footwork and suggested that the greater of the mountain ranges be called "The Coyotes." All of the animals laughed to see him in good spirits again. Turtle waved a flipper toward the desert land to the northeast and said, "I think I see Coyote's first paw mark out there. When the rains come, it will fill with water. Shall we call it Coyote Lake?" There was great laughter, and it was decided that it should be so. And so it is.

Since the earth at last was dry, Chief Eagle and Coyote then began to send the animals out to their homes on the new land. To the bears they said, "You go with your people to the mountains there, and over here, and out yonder." The deer they sent to meadows, the beavers to streams, some animals to springs and others to caves and canyons. Each one of the animal folk thanked Eagle and then headed for his new home. Already grass was sprouting and trees were growing, and the land promised many good things.

Soon no one was left but Eagle and Coyote, and for a while they stayed on the Lonely Mountain and looked out across California. "Where will you go?" asked Coyote of Eagle.

"I have been trying to decide," said Eagle. "I think

I shall go up there." He waved his wing toward the sky. "Just to keep an eye on things for a while."

"But what of me?" Coyote said. "Where do I go?"

"You may have this mountain," answered Eagle.

"Alone? No, I shall go with you."

"No, Coyote. You must stay here below. Someone must look after this place, and you are the only one left." They argued and argued until finally Eagle would have no more of it. "Good-by," he said, and off he flew.

"Wait for me!" yelped Coyote. "I am coming too!"

Eagle called back from on high, "You cannot. You do not have wings. Choose your own place to live if you wish, but you cannot come with me!"

"I will!" cried Coyote, and he gave a great leap into the air. But it was of no use. He only fell from the rocks and rolled down the mountainside in a great clatter of stones and a cloud of dust. "Well," he said, picking himself up and brushing the dust from his fur, "I wouldn't have cared for it up there. I think I'll have a look around down here instead."

And so he trotted off.

The Securing of Light

NE time after the world had settled and grown comfortable and Coyote had found himself a wife and sons, it happened that the grass and trees and flowers stopped growing because the night lasted all day. No one noticed at first. Because there was no light, the birds did not awaken at all (except for Owl, who was quite happy about it), and the animals, whose minds were taken up with other things, did not bother to think about it until Ho, the Polecat, fell in the river in the dark. Even then they were not sure what was wrong. Since it was night, perhaps they were dreaming. But as the world grew colder and yet colder and the night showed no sign of ending, they knew that someone had stolen the sun. The grass shriveled and flowers drooped, and the animals saw that without the sun everything, even themselves, must die.

"Who has taken it? Where has it gone?" they cried, and no one knew the answers. Coyote was no help, for shivering, his teeth chattering, he had only burrowed more deeply into his bed with a muffled "Wake me when you have found it again." However, when the sounds of their worried argument had faded into the distance, Coyote found that he could not sleep for the cold. Something had to be done.

"It is because my head is cold," he thought. "We must be facing the north wind." And so he roused his wife, telling her to turn herself and the pups to face the west. When he, too, had turned, he settled down for a good sleep, only to find that his head was as cold as before. "Wife," he said, "get up. We shall feel less of a draft if we turn to the south." But once turned, he found it as cold as before. "Wife," Coyote chattered, "it is an ill wind that blows from the east, but since it cannot be any colder than this, we might as well try turning again." And so they did, curling up once more. Coyote had very nearly dropped off to sleep before he realized that his head was now quite warm.

"But my tail is still quite cold," he pondered. "Perhaps the sun has been taken off to the east. In that case, I must go and fetch it back." He yawned. "I shall think about it for a while first. Then I shall go." And he drifted off to sleep.

When he awoke, the sky was still as black as pitch, but he felt his way downhill to the next lodge, hoping to find a companion for his journey to the east. "Whose house is this?" called Coyote, and from inside Mole answered, "Mine."

"Mole? No, I do not want you. You like the darkness. I want someone to help me fetch the sun so that we may have light." Coyote groped his way to the next lodge, where he found Deermouse. "You must be my dog, friend Deermouse," he said. "I am going to the east to fetch back the sun, and you have a good nose for sniffing out the best trail. Will you and your brother come?"

The Deermice readily agreed, and they set off without delay. "I fear it will be a far journey," said Coyote, "for night stretches as far as I can see." And far it was. Hour after hour the Deermice scampered on with Coyote padding at their heels until at last hunger made the poor mice stagger. Coyote was alarmed. "Are you hungry?" he asked. "What can I get for you? A bit of good meat? I could hunt up a juicy squirrel if you wish. What will you have?"

"No, no squirrel." The elder Deermouse looked pained. "An acorn or two, perhaps a head of clover, will suit us well." And the mice lay back against a tuft of dry grass until Coyote returned with three acorns, five pine nuts, and seven walnuts.

When the mice had eaten their fill, he finished off the remaining walnuts himself and then said, "Come, we must make tracks."

On they went, over ridges and across valleys. They came to a river where the water was so swift that the Deermice feared they should be swept away; and though Coyote coaxed them to swim, they would not and finally rode across clinging to his fur. Once upon the other side, they traveled swiftly across a wide land until the younger Deermouse at last stumbled from weariness. "I be tired," he mumbled. "I rest here. I lie down. Please?" Coyote and the elder Deermouse ached for a rest as well, and so all three stretched out beside the trail. While they lay there, Coyote sang a song, a song he had learned as a pup—

"Light. Hayolkal. In the house made of light.
Light. Hayolkal. Being made of light.
Light. Hayolkal. With a trail marked by light."

"What means your song, friend Coyote?" asked the Deermice.

"What does it mean? Oh, nothing. I heard it from a strange chicken hawk, if I remember. It makes no sense to me," said he. "Come, we must set off again. I am sure that we must be close, for my tail is warm again. Your feet—are they rested?"

"Yes," they said, "but let us walk rather than run.

We have come such a long way and may yet have far to go." Reluctantly Coyote agreed, for he did not care to go on alone. Warmer and warmer grew the air and thirstier grew the travelers. When they came upon a shallow stream, they paused to drink, noses in the water, tongues lapping.

"We must be nearly there, my dogs," said Coyote, licking the last drops of water from his whiskers. "I think that I see a light yonder. Take care that you go quietly, and follow me." They crept, bellies low to the ground. At the top of a low rise, they came upon the source of the light. It was not the sun. Someone had built a fire at the base of a thick-waisted oak tree, and the fire had run up the trunk, turning the branches into a torch that lit the countryside for miles about. Two small figures danced around the torch tree.

"Who are they?" whispered the mice to Coyote, who crouched behind a manzanita bush, peering through the branches.

"One seems to be Lizard. And the other, I fear, is Mole. He thinks to trick me, for he is happy without the sun. Lizard must have come along to warm himself by the fire, but Mole is up to some trickery. I am sure of it. He would say, 'Ho, Coyote! I see that you, too, have felt the heat and have come to warm yourself by this great fire.' But he will not fool me. The sun is hidden not far from here. Mole's trick makes me certain of it. Come. They have not seen us. If we creep back the way we came, then circle widely around them, we can be safely on our way."

So they did. Scarcely had they circled to the far side of the wide pool of firelight when they caught sight of what appeared to be a light from a distant window spilling onto a distant path.

"Ho, ho!" Coyote chuckled, quite pleased with himself, as they trotted toward the glow. "It is as I said. Coyote is no pup to be fooled by such as Mole." Upon drawing near to the bright lodge, he motioned with a paw for the mice to halt. Heat, thick and heavy, poured from window, door, and smoke hole of the lodge. There was the sound of old women's voices. "Stay here, my dogs," Coyote cautioned the mice. "I shall take a look."

From below the window Coyote raised first his nose, then eyes and ears over the sill. Two ugly old women—wrinkled, straggly locked, and filthy—sat talking with their backs to him. In the middle of the floor, directly beneath the smoke hole, was the sun, tied down with leather straps and covered with a blanket. Coyote grinned with satisfaction and turned back to rejoin the Deermice.

"The lodge is empty but for the sun and two old toothless ones who guard it. If they were to sleep, if I could but make them fall into a deep sleep, you could easily chew through the straps with which they have bound the sun, and I could carry it off. Yes, that is the best of all possible plans." And carefully he directed the Deermice when and how to creep in and where to chew the sun's leather bonds. He also told them that they should nudge him with their noses when they had finished, taking care to make no noise.

Setting them to wait in the shadows beside the door, Coyote knocked loudly upon the door, crying, "Hai, good folk within! I am a weary traveler in need of a bed. Can you not shelter me for the night?" The door opened a crack, and Coyote staggered against it, stumbling inside before the old women could gather their wits. "Thank you, my grandmothers," he moaned. "I have no strength for food. A bed is all I want."

Amazed, the two old women stared at each other and then at Coyote, who had crept to a pallet lying by the wall close by the doorway. "Might I have a blanket, grandmothers?" he groaned, shivering and looking quite ill.

"I suppose there is no harm in it," grumbled one old woman to the other. "It would not do to turn such a sickling out."

Muttering, the second old woman stooped to twitch the blanket from the sun and throw it over

Coyote. "There." She sniffed. "But I tell you I do not like the looks of him at all. And without the blanket, the sun is too bright for us to keep an eye on it, so we had best watch this moth-eaten fellow instead."

Drawing the blanket over his head, Coyote pretended that he had heard nothing, and as the toothless ones settled back to watch, he began very softly to murmur, "Sleep, sleep, sleepy. You sleep. You sleep."

"What might that noise be?" hissed the first old woman.

"I do not know," said the other. "I never heard such a sound before. Perhaps it is the sun sighing in its sleep."

"Sleepy. So sleepy. Sleep. You sleep. Sleep," droned Coyote.

"No, it is not the sun." The first old woman yawned. "It is that fellow yonder under the blanket."

The second rubbed her eyes and padded to Coyote's side. "Who are you? What is it that you say, grandson? The sound of it makes us fear."

Coyote raised the blanket and opened one eye. "Ah, I was only dreaming, old grandmother. I have traveled far through many lands and am weary, am tired . . . am sleepy. Sleepy. Sleep, sleep, you sleep, you sleep." As he dropped the blanket over his head, the old women rubbed their eyes with their fists and yawned widely. For a space of some minutes—perhaps fifteen or twenty—Coyote murmured gently, over and over and over, the drowsy words.

At first the old ones stretched, tried to smother their yawns, and blinked heavy eyes. Then sitting down, backs to the wall, they tried to hold their eyes open with their fingers. This failing, their chins drooped onto their chests. After a nervous twitch or two, both began to snore. Coyote, not daring to move, continued his sleepy chant. Not until he felt several sharp pokes upon his ribs did he know whether his plan had worked.

The Deermice pointed silently to the dangling ends of the straps about the sun. They had left two pieces long enough for Coyote to use as handles, and so, as they skittered through the door, Coyote was close behind, lugging the sun. "Hurry!" he whispered. "We must hurry!"

Up rise and down arroyo they ran. They made good speed, far better than they had made in coming, for the sun—though weak and still bound about with thongs—threw off light enough to brighten even the distant hills. Yet that light which sped their feet brought ill luck when it caught and dazzled the eyes of Mole and Lizard. Lizard was secretly happy to see that the sun had been freed, for he missed basking in the sunshine on warm rocks; but his friend Mole was angered. The sun dazzled and pained his eyes, and he

had hoped that the old women might at least have had time to weaken it, to make it pale and puny. "It is Coyote!" he howled. "Coyote is carrying off the sun! I will not have it! Why must he always poke his nose where it is not wanted?"

Mole picked up a large stick and ran toward the lodge from which Coyote had taken the sun. With it he beat upon the wall until the house boomed like a drum. "Awake!" he shrieked to the dazed hags. "Awake! Coyote has made off with the sun! Awake!"

And they did—opening their eyes, peering about in astonishment, then yelling with fury. With whoops and bellowings, they rushed from the lodge to streak after the retreating sunlight.

Coyote heard them coming from afar. Their wrath was terrible in his ears. "Run faster, my little dogs," he panted to the Deermice, who had begun to fall behind. "The old hags run swiftly in our tracks."

"But we be so tired!" gasped the mice.

Coyote, too, was tiring, for the sun seemed to grow heavier and brighter with each step he took. "Take heart," he wheezed, "for we are but a little way from the hilltop lodge called Yelindun, where we shall be safe. It is yonder above Blackwater Creek."

They ran, stumbling, up the hill called Yalcul-saik'wut, which from its summit sloped down to the creek. As they crossed the bare rock slope that led to the top, shouts rang up from below. "We see you, moth-eaten ones!" shrilled the old women. "Stop! Give us back our sun. We have not finished fixing it. Give it back!" They waved scrawny arms, scrambling up the path as they shouted.

Turning, Coyote called, "Oh yes, I am sure you mean to fix it—fix it so that it will not shine. And you were not hiding it, of course—not a bit!" Holding the sun carefully, he looked about until he saw a large speckled green stone on the ground ahead. "Hei, hai!" He laughed, beckoning the Deermice out of harm's way. "This will serve them!" And with his foot he sent the green rock rolling down the trail. It bounded and bounced, bearing swiftly down upon the hags; and though they turned to flee, it was no use. The first old woman it hit upon the ankle and the second upon the elbow, and both were turned to stone. Their stone eyes stared, and their stone feet were rooted to the ground. Their stone tongues could not wag, and their stone mouths were silent.

For the mice and Coyote, there was no longer need to hurry. Over the crest, downhill, across the shallows of Blackwater Creek, and upwards to Yelindun they trudged. The lodge was a welcome sight and good shelter should Mole by any chance come nosing about. The Deermice stretched out to rest in a tule basket lying in the shade, and Coyote set to work.

From the lodge he fetched a large obsidian knife. Behind the lodge he found a great shallow stone metate. Taking out its stone pestle, he set the sun in its bowl and cut the leather thongs that had bound it. Brightly it glared. Then, shielding his eyes, Coyote began to cut the sun into bits and slices. When he had trimmed off one largish bit, a goodish pile of small bits, and a fair slice, he was satisfied. "Now we will have something to give light on our trails at night," he said.

"This," he said, picking up the largish bit, "shall be called Atcegegutcuk, the Morning Star; and it shall warn us of the coming sun." After looking about the sky, he took great care and hurled Atcegegutcuk into place above the horizon. It held firmly to the sky.

"And now for Sunlantc!" The large ball left on the metate after trimming he thrust with all his strength into the western sky, where it hung securely, moving by degrees toward the Coast Range and the ocean beyond. It cast bright daylight upon the westernmost lands and shone in the streams, but soon it dipped behind the mountain range and was gone before any creature had crept outdoors to see it.

Quickly Coyote gathered the smaller bits to cast them in handfuls everywhere about the night sky until trees and rocks and ridges could be seen by starlight. "It is good," said Coyote. "But these stars are scarcely bright enough for night hunting. It will be many hours before Sunlantc circles to the east to begin another day." He spied the last of the pieces cut from the sun, a slice that lay propped against the wall of the lodge. It had grown quite cool but still shone silver, if not the white gold it had been.

"The very thing! This I shall call Moon, and it shall roll across the night sky." With a swing of his arm, he spun it into the star-speckled sky, and the job was finished. He called out to the mice, who roused themselves to admire his handiwork. However, upon his proposal that they should return home in his company, they begged to be excused and returned yawning to their basket bed.

And so it was that Coyote trotted home alone to slip into the bed he had left so many hours before. His wife and pups snored contentedly, and scarcely had Coyote stretched out before his snores were joined in the chorus.

An hour before dawn he felt a poking in his ribs. "Father, Father!" cried the youngest pup. "There is a small bright thing hanging in the sky above the hills. What shall we do?"

"Go back to sleep," mumbled Coyote. "It is only the Morning Star. I put it there. It will not harm you."

Just after dawn the second youngest pup poked

Coyote with his nose. "Oh, Father, Father! There is a sun in the sky, and it does not look like the old one. What shall we do?"

"Go out to play and leave me to sleep," grumbled Coyote. "It is the same old sun. I have only pared it down a little." And he turned over to sleep the rest of the day away.

Not long after sunset the next to oldest pup nudged him sharply. "Father, oh, Father!" he cried. "The night sky is ill and speckled with spots, and the sun has fallen out of the sky! What shall we do?"

"Go to bed." Coyote groaned. "The sun has gone to bed but will rise again tomorrow over the Sierras. Those are stars in the sky, not spots. I put them there myself. I should know. Get you to bed." Coyote rolled over and curled up warmly between his wife and the pups.

Hardly had they settled when the eldest pup jumped upon Coyote, crying, "Father, Father, awake! A great silver face hangs in the dark sky. Let us flee before we are eaten!"

In his sleep Coyote murmured, "Lie down, lie down. It is only the Moon. It cannot bite. I made it. I should know."

On the following day Coyote slept still while his wife and his pups explained to the animal folk about the Sun, the Moon, and the Stars. But everyone laughed at them. "What?" they cried, holding their sides with laughter. "Coyote rescue the sun? He who is too lazy to haul himself from bed? He who always speaks of great things but never does them?" They joked about Coyote's blunders and his vanity until the pups began to wail and Coyote's wife to weep.

So great was the clamor that the Deermice, now returning, ran the last mile to the village in order the sooner to see what had caused such noise. When they had told their tale of the securing of light, the coyotes cheered and the others were amazed. Being generous at heart, all rushed to Coyote's lodge to awaken him with thanks and a great clapping of paws.

Coyote, dignified, appeared in the doorway. "It was nothing," he said with a wave of the paw.

But he was glad when they loudly disagreed.

The Theft of Dawn

SOME moons after the sun had been replaced in its path across the sky, word came to Eagle and to Lone Wolf that the animals were not happy with Coyote's work. They claimed that if they did not happen to awaken in time to glimpse the Morning Star, they were rudely startled when the sun popped up over the eastern hills. Up it leaped, glaring fiercely and dazzling the eyes of anyone who happened to be facing east at the moment of sunrise. Was there not some way of warning folk so that there would be no need of stumbling about, sun-blind, for half the morning?

Eagle and Lone Wolf called a council to which came the animals from all of the surrounding valleys. After much palaver, Antelope—who often traveled great distances into other lands—reported that he had once heard of a place to the east where daylight crept across the sky before the sun appeared above the hills. "But that was long ago," he said, "and I have heard nothing of it since the sun was stolen and rescued again by our brother, Coyote."

"Perhaps someone has stolen that light as well," mused Eagle. "It must be so. It may be hidden somewhere there to the east."

"Shall we send a fast runner eastward to spy it out?" asked Lone Wolf.

At this all of the animals cried, "Yes!"

"Let it be Blue Jay," said one, "for he is more swift than the eye. He can outrun the wind." And all agreed.

Blue Jay, proud of being chosen scout, thanked his people and asked whether it would not be wise for him to take a companion in case the early daylight be found and prove too heavy for one alone to carry. It was agreed, and Ground Squirrel was proposed as an assistant carrier-of-the-load.

Both scouts adorned themselves with strings of beads and shells so that, if seen, they should seem innocent and prosperous travelers to the east. So as not to be seen, they traveled under the moon, sleeping during the day in safe thickets along the wayside. Eastward for several nights they went, but nowhere

did they see daylight coming gently before the sun. Everywhere, as in their own land, the sun burst suddenly over the horizon, blinding the unwary. It was not until five suns and five moons had risen and set, not until they had pierced deeply into a land near the edge of the world, that the walkers-under-the-moon saw the sky pale, saw the clouds above the horizon glow with pink and gold, and saw the sun bound up into a sky already blue.

"How beautiful! How gentle! It should be so in our land as well," chattered Ground Squirrel.

Blue Jay had already flown high with a beating of wings to spy out lodges and villages, if any there were. In a moment he plummeted down to Ground Squirrel's side. "Friend Squirrel," he said, "there is a great village beyond this hillock at whose base we stand. Yet in it there are no fires. No dogs bark, and no old women chatter or grind maize in the metates. Yet it seems a rich village."

"I do not understand," blinked Ground Squirrel. "Is it that we have almost walked into a deserted village?"

"So my eyes and ears would tell me. Let us together approach more closely—but silently, lest these be people who sleep in the daylight." Such would be difficult to believe, and Ground Squirrel laughed at the idea.

Even at the edge of the village, no sound came to their ears, and so they determined to investigate more fully once the sun had set. The village indeed was rich. There were many lodges roofed and walled with thickly woven mats whereon yellow suns shone, blue waters ran, and painted hunters stalked. Painted pots and carved metates rested beside each door. Even the racks where thin strips of meat hung to dry were brightly colored and decked with feathers and strings of clamshells, as were the doorposts. All of the village paths led inward to a great earth lodge in the center, the most splendid the travelers had ever seen.

At dusk the door was still unguarded, and they hesitated but a moment before slipping into the great lodge. Immediately there came to their ears a short squeal of fright, followed by a smothered sniffle. In the dim light there could be seen a wide bare floor, a great firepit, and numerous storage baskets lined against the walls. Sitting atop a basket by the far wall was a boy no taller than a mouse's ears, his face covered with his hands.

Blue Jay moved across the earthen floor. "Hai, young one!" he said in greeting. "How is it that you are alone? We are travelers and had thought to pay our respects to your chief, to smoke a pipe with him."

Peering through his fingers, the boy answered, "All

are gone. There is a dance in the village nearest here, but I am too small to walk so far."

"It is a great pity"—Blue Jay nodded politely—"for there is nothing more pleasant than to dance the night through." Now that his eyes were accustomed to the darkness, he looked about with interest. The small boy, having taken heart at the kind words, no longer hid his face but watched Blue Jay and Ground Squirrel openly. Despite his smallness he was a well-formed boy, in no way unusual except for his face, which was exceedingly ugly. His eyes were black and round and very bright, his nose was hardly to be seen, and his mouth seemed to stretch from ear to ear. Blue Jay thought it odd that a village should be abandoned to the protection of such a minnow.

"And what," said he, "might be in that basket yonder, Small Brave?" He pointed to the first of those along the south wall.

"It is naught but buttercup seeds," answered the child warily.

"And that?"

"Only sunflower seeds."

"And the one beyond?"

"It is nothing. Only shooting stars. That is all."

"And here?"

"Merely black oak acorns."

For a long while Blue Jay questioned the boy,

pointing to each basket and learning which ones contained tule seeds, clamshells, or pine nuts, and which held obsidian, mesquite beans, or milkweed pods. Though the eyes of the small boy glittered with suspicion, he did not hesitate in his answers. When there was but one basket yet unnamed, Blue Jay with a friendly smile said, "Hei, hai! I had almost forgotten! What fills the basket whereupon you sit?"

"Dawn," said the boy, unblinking.

Whereupon Blue Jay dashed forward, thrusting the boy aside. He seized the basket, leaped for the door, and flew into the darkness. Just as quickly, Ground Squirrel swung a large chunk of obsidian onto his back and scurried away, carrying a basket of sunflower seeds under one arm and one of acorns under the other.

Yet all was not well. At the moment of Blue Jay's first step forward, the child had opened wide the mouth that stretched from ear to ear and shouted in a thunderous voice, "My people! My people! Our Dawn is being stolen. Thief-with-wings is taking our Dawn!" Miles away, where the villagers danced to drums and rattles, no one paid heed. As Ground Squirrel disappeared into the darkness with his loot, the boy opened wide his mouth again, crying, "My people, come! Our Dawn is gone. Thief-with-whiskers has carried off many riches. Oh, Dawn People, come!"

One dancer harkened at last. "Big Mouth calls us!" he cried to the dancers. The drums stopped. "The boy shouts that our Dawn has been stolen. Swiftly must we follow."

Big Mouth met his people at the edge of their village to point out the direction in which Blue Jay had flown. Ground Squirrel had gone another way; yet as acorns, sunflower seeds, and obsidian could be more easily replaced than the Dawn, no one followed him. Everyone pursued Blue Jay. Though he was well ahead, the Dawn People soon drew nearer, following westward the pale glow of Dawn that leaked from around the top of the basket. Their feet were swift and their legs were strong, and unlike Blue Jay, they had no heavy loads to slow them. Stride by stride they lessened the gap as the Dawn basket light streamed low across the sky.

So swiftly flew Blue Jay that by the end of night he had traveled almost as far as on all of the nights of the eastward journey together. The Dawn People, angered beyond measure by the loss of their treasured Dawn, were yet more swift. The heat of their breath warmed Blue Jay's feathers, and the beating of his wings began to falter. At Big Valley, only an arrow's flight from the villages of home, they overtook him.

But if no longer fleet of feather, Blue Jay was yet nimble of wit. At the very moment of his falling, before he was surrounded and seized, he tore the woven lid from the basket. The Dawn poured out, spreading westward over the hills and ridges; and the Dawn People wailed and tore at their hair to see it freed. No thought gave they to Blue Jay, who slipped away in the confusion of their grief and anger. But a few miles' flight and he dropped wearily upon the smokehouse roof of his own village.

"Hei, hai!" shouted Coyote from his lodge across the way. "Blue Jay has returned. And the Dawn comes with him! Arise, my people!" And all came out to see, watching with Blue Jay as the clouds of the lightening sky grew pink and then were washed with gold. Brightly shone the crests of the eastern hills at the moment before the sun's edge slid into sight.

"Ahhh!" breathed all of the animals. "It is a *great* improvement!" And Blue Jay was congratulated heartily by Eagle, Lone Wolf, and Coyote.

"But what has befallen friend Ground Squirrel?" Eagle asked. "He, too, has earned thanks for this brave raid."

At which all began to wonder and talk among themselves, fearing that ill had overtaken Ground Squirrel, that excellent burden-bearer who, after all, did have very short legs. No sooner had they fallen still with the fear that he had been trapped and torn to pieces by the Dawn People than Ground Squirrel himself appeared on the trail that led to the village. His acorns and sunflower seeds were gratefully received, and Ground Squirrel was loudly acclaimed.

"Here," said he, rolling the obsidian from his back. "Take this as well. Such black stone makes fine tools. But ai! My back is blistered from the carrying of it, such sharp edges it has."

And it is for this reason that Ground Squirrel has stripes upon his back, for where the blisters had been, his fur grew as black as obsidian.

Cottontail and the Sun

I N the early days the sun was extremely hot. Cottontail, who lived at Black Rock, could scarcely bear the heat that beat into his small cave in the rocks. "The sun," he said, "is just too hot!" At last he determined to find out why the sun blazed so cruelly, to see, if such were possible, what might be done about it. And so one day, before dawn, he packed up a bit of food and his arrows, slung his bow over his shoulder, and set off to find the home of Sun. It was, he thought, atop the mountain to the east.

But once atop the mountain to the east, Cottontail saw that Sun had already climbed from his bed and glared hotly in the sky above the next mountain eastward. "Ha!" said Cottontail. "I shall have to rise earlier tomorrow morning. Then I shall be able to reach his home before he hops into the sky."

The following morning Cottontail set out while it was yet dark, but when he topped the ridge of the second mountain, he saw that Sun had already risen. The third morning it was the same. And the fourth. Each time that Cottontail felt sure he had found Sun's home, Sun appeared above the mountain just beyond. Mountain after mountain Cottontail crossed until at the last he came to a great ocean and could go no further. Sun was nowhere to be seen.

Patient Cottontail searched along the shore until he found a snug rocky cave. Bow and arrow in hand, he lay in wait in the mouth of the cave. "Sun shall not slip past me this time," he vowed. That very moment, almost catching him unawares, Sun hopped up from the ocean, shaking himself and steaming hotly.

Cottontail shot. Sun came tumbling down to land in the sand with a "thunk." Swiftly Cottontail whipped out his packet of food, chose a piece of liver, sliced it in slices thin as a butterfly's wing, and pasted them all over the face of Sun. When he turned his back to pick up the last sliver of liver, Sun's uncovered spot blazed out, scorching Cottontail's back. Angrily Cottontail slapped the last piece of liver into place and shoved Sun back into the sky.

Since that day the sun has not shone so fiercely as in the first days of the world—and Cottontail has the mark upon his back to prove it.

The Theft of Fire

N the first days there was no fire. Oh, indeed, the folk had fire of a sort, but it was not hot enough to burn truly. It did not even blister when one touched it, and its flames were paler than moonlight now is. Still, for a long while no one minded.

The stronger menfolk went about their business hunting deer so that their families might have full bellies and warm deerskin-blanketed beds. The smaller folk and oldsters wove fine nets to catch fine salmon, and the womenfolk and children made baskets for the gathering of sunflower seeds. There was no lack of food. Yet each evening as the venison was taken from the roasting fire, few were the grins of pleasure and the lickings of chops, for the meat was only greasily warm. On days when the nets were heavy with salmon, days that could have meant a rich feast, there was no great rejoicing. The fish were fetched back to the village, were split and cleaned and spread on the cooking rocks in the midst of the fire, and were eaten; but there was no joy in the eating. It was still raw fish just as the venison had been raw deer. Even the sunflower seeds that the women put on the cooking stones to brown and roast barely became warm. They were hard to chew and bitter to the taste.

The menfolk among the animals were first to tire of the tasteless food. "Hei, hai!" They spat. "This fire we use is useless! It were better to eat meat freshly killed and still warm or fish still cold from the stream than this. We are tired of raw food; our jaws are tired from the chewing of it." Their wives agreed helplessly but knew of no way of preparing food so that it might be more pleasant to eat.

"Heh!" muttered one who stood on a cooking stone to warm his feet a bit. "What we need is hotter fire."

"But where should we find such a thing?" asked another.

"Perchance," replied the first, who was Lone Wolf, "there may be such fire hereabouts. Never have we looked far. There may be such to the east beyond the mountains; perchance there, to the south; or yonder to the west; or even to the north."

This speech caused great excitement. "Let us search to see if there be such fire!" many cried, and a council was called for that night so that plans for the search might be made. Word was sent out for all to come—all but Coyote, for Lone Wolf did not want Coyote, who wished always to be in charge, to direct and manage and muddle every plan. And while the runners gathered the folk, Lone Wolf and several others stepped outside of the evening fire's pale ring of light so that they might see whether any distant fire glowed in the twilight.

"A darkness has crept over the rim of the eastern mountains," said one of his companions. "From there we should better be able to see if fire gleams against the blackness."

"Yes," said Lone Wolf. "But it is far, and we must soon return for the council. The mountain to our north is closer, and by the time of our reaching it, the darkness will have washed westward across the whole of the land. If there be fire hereabouts, we will see it from there."

So they set their feet upon the trail and went. The dusk thickened about their ankles, and to the right hand—from the east—blackness grew in the manzanita trees so that even the mountains were no longer to be seen. The animals hurried, climbing swiftly until they topped the small mountain and could catch their breath. Shining dimly to the south was the feeble fire they had left below. Into the eastern darkness Lone Wolf peered, but no fire was to be seen there, nor was there any to the north. To the west there was no light but the last lingering of sunset. "Hei, hai!" he exclaimed. "The east and north and west are dark, and no light but our own poor fire gleams to the south."

Again they looked on all sides, but it was when at last they turned their noses unhappily toward the south and the trail home that Lone Wolf spied a prick of light far beyond their own cold pale fire. "I cannot tell," he muttered, straining his eyes, "but it seems too low to be a star."

"Where? Where?" chorused his companions. And at the moment of their asking, the answer blazed up brightly in the distance. With a great shower of sparks it flamed up, fell, roared up, and again died down. So bright it was that afterwards, upon looking for the flickering flames of their village fire, the animals could see nothing until they had rubbed the dazzle from their eyes. Excitement hastened their homeward steps, the steep trail tilted them downwards in leaps and scrambles, and many a tuft of fur was left in snags on the grasping buckthorn bushes.

Upon their arrival in the village, all of the animal folk joined them in the smokehouse to sit in formal council. When Lone Wolf and his companions saw the fire tender toss a great log onto the smokehouse fire, they watched the chilly sparks billow like a shadow cloud of smoke and they laughed. When each animal had taken his seat, Lone Wolf stepped forward to tell them of the great fire, as much hotter than this they sat by as the sun is hotter than the moon. Though it was as far away as the point where the earth meets the sky, one could see the billowing sparks when the faraway fire tender fed it logs. "Not like this!" He laughed, pointing.

Where was it? Was it really so far? How long a journey? Could they not steal a piece of it? Who was to go? The questions flew. Within a short time it was decided that a piece of the far-off fire must be stolen and that Lone Wolf should lead the raid.

"Who are the best of runners?" asked Lone Wolf. "Who loves to run? For we shall need the speed of wind." Fox thrust forward eagerly, and Lone Wolf grinned. "Yes, Wus shall come. He is fast in running but faster yet in cunning. Who shall be his second? Who can skim the earth with swiftest feet?" Sandpiper raised his wing, and Lone Wolf, thinking it good that one of the raiders be able to fly, bade him come to stand beside Fox. "It is good," he said. "These two, Wus and Aiwia-oona, shall come with me, as will Mole, who sees well in the darkness, and Weasel, who moves without sound." The council agreed that his choices were wise.

It was also thought wise that the five raiders should depart at once so that they might have the cover of darkness both going and returning. And so they did. They were well away before the last of their council had left the smokehouse. At Mole's suggestion the adventurers made the first part of their journey underground by way of one of his many tunnels, so that no outsider might wonder at seeing five shadows slip from the village so late at night.

The tunnel ended at the side of a stream now known as Battle Creek, and from there the journey south was made under the wide sky, which was scarcely lighter than the tunnel. Yet that faint lightness brought their first ill luck. Had Mole's tunnel come up beyond the stream, all would have been well. Coyote would not have seen them. Coyote was visiting with his mother's sister's cousin's people, whose lodges bordered the creek; and through a chink in the wall, he saw five black shadows steal across the lighter shadow that was the water. Ill luck indeed!

"Aha!" exclaimed Coyote. "Someone is up to something! Arise, my mother's sister's cousin's people!

Five shadows have crossed your creek. Who might they be and where might they be going?"

"We know not," they grumbled sleepily.

Coyote was not content. He peered out of the door-way and called to a rock that sat at the water's edge. "Ho, rock!" he cried. "Tell me where those folk were going at such an hour as this,"—to which the rock's answer was a grumbling "I know not," followed by a stony silence. The cooking basket that hung by the door gave the same answer to his demand, as did the house itself. "We saw no one," they grumped sleepily.

Coyote spied a brush for sifting acorn flour hang-ing from the branch of a tree near the water. "Ho, brush!" he called. "Where were those five night runners going?" The brush, angry at having been awakened by Coyote's loud curiosity, sought to quiet him by replying, "They have gone to hunt deer. It is nothing. Go back to sleep."

But Coyote was not to be left out of a hunt. "Hai!" he muttered. "They should have told me. Why, I wonder, did they not tell me? Everyone knows I am best at deer tracking. They will never have any luck without me. I must find them and lend a hand." And so he set off to the east, thinking to catch them up in no time. An hour had passed before he realized that at each turning of the dark paths he had bent to the left and come again full circle to the lodges of his mother's sister's cousin's folk. By then the five raiders were many miles away, but Coyote was determined that they should have his help as no one else could track deer so well as he.

He stumbled over an acorn mortar left by the stream bank after the acorn grinding of the day now long gone. "Aiee!" he moaned, and then he bethought himself that perhaps he had not been the only one to stumble there. "Ho, acorn metate! Some time ago five shadows crossed the creek. They must have passd by you. Tell me: where were they going in such a soft-footed fashion?"

The metate yawned. "South. South. They all went south," and promptly returned to its sleep.

"So!" mused Coyote. "South. Yes. But are there deer to the south? No matter: it is my duty to go and lend a hand." So he set off again, running down the southern trail. The five hunters (as he supposed them to be) now traveled slowly, saving their strength for the long race home—as they knew it to be unlikely that the southern fire owners would give up even one coal without a chase. Thus it was that Coyote caught up with them.

"Ho there!" he cried when he thought he glimpsed them on the trail ahead. "Ho there! Wait for me, I pray!"

And they, fearful that he should awaken the whole countryside, halted until he came abreast of them. "Oh, salmon bones!" Lone Wolf groaned as he recognized the ears and wagging tail. "It is Coyote. He has followed us."

"Hoo!" panted Coyote as he trotted up. "Hard work, this running in the dark. But you are lucky that I found you. You really should have sent me word. Ah, Lone Wolf! And who else? Fox? And Sandpiper? Mole? Weasel? Are we all here? Where are we off to?"

Being quite angry and thinking it better to say nothing than to speak their minds, the five spoke not a word. Turning their noses south once more, they set off at a brisk jog. Coyote, at their heels, supposed that the silence must mean they were close to some new hunting grounds. Not until they came in sight of a cluster of lodges lit by the light that poured from the smoke hole and doorway of a great hilltop sweathouse did he realize his mistake. This was no deer hunt.

Pausing outside the ring of light, Lone Wolf whispered directions to his companions. Coyote he ignored altogether. Mole was sent to peer into the nearest, darkest lodge.

"You should have sent me," whispered Coyote. "Mole is a good fellow, but he has hard work to see the nose on front of his face." The others pretended not to hear. Within moments Mole had nosed his way back to the group.

"They are the Wind People, the children of the winds," he said. "Even asleep, they make the lodge tremble with their sighs."

"Tso, tso!" mused Lone Wolf. "That is why they could breed so strong a fire. They can huff and puff at coals and yet never be short of breath. But we must tread carefully. It would not do to have such folk as these too soon upon our trail." With these and more words of caution, he sent Weasel and Fox to the sweathouse roof to spy out the lay of the fire. Many Wind Folk there were stretched out upon the floor and snoring loudly. The fire had died to a great heap of redly glowing coals and brands, but though it was directly below the smoke hole, neither Wus the Fox nor Weasel could reach it. Their companions on the ground waited fearfully.

"You ought to have told me what it was that wanted doing." Coyote sighed. "By now we would be well away. Wus and Weasel mean well, but they are bound to go at it the wrong way." The others paid no attention.

Soon Wus and Weasel had found a way. With Weasel on the roof, clutching the fox's bushy tail, Wus was able to hang headfirst down through the

smoke hole and to snatch a brand from the fire. Silently Weasel tugged him back through the hole, and they leaped to the ground. With Wus running ahead, the five raiders and Coyote dashed for the northward trail.

Coyote was everywhere at once. "Run, everyone, run!" he panted. "Don't talk—save your breath," he wheezed. "And if you tire, throw the fire to me, and I shall make for home."

Northwards they flew, moving smoothly while Coyote scrambled behind. At the place known now as Mill Creek, Wus tossed the fire to Sandpiper, who moved into the lead. "Oh!" cried Coyote. "You should have given it to me. I can carry it in my paw. When he carries it in his mouth that way, how is he to call out for help?" He tried to push past Wus the Fox to beg the fire from Sandpiper.

"Look out!" snapped Wus. "And keep back. Were you to carry it in your paw, you would burn yourself. You would drop the fire."

Coyote looked deeply offended. "For what did I come south? I felt it my duty to come, to make sure your venture succeeded. What am I to say when our folk ask, 'And you, Coyote, what did you do?' How can I answer 'Nothing'—I, Coyote? No! I shall say, 'I bore you fire in my paw—I, Coyote!'"

They had reached Battle Creek. Short-legged Mole

had fallen far behind, and Weasel held back to keep him company. Lone Wolf ran steadily, watching over his shoulder for signs of pursuit; and Coyote kept abreast of Wus only with the greatest of effort. "Please let me carry the fire," he pleaded of Sandpiper, who flapped on just ahead of his nose.

At last Sandpiper was forced to toss the brand to Wus. It was too heavy for such a small bird to carry far. The fox in turn, sure that they were too close to home for any harm to be done, cried from between his clenched teeth, "Hold out your paw. Here! Take it and have done!" Coyote reached out to catch the flying fire, and both Sandpiper and Wus stopped to wait for Lone Wolf. Had they kept on, it would have been better, for Coyote did burn his paw and did drop the fire, and as he hopped up and down crying, "Aiee! Du, du, du, du-du-du!" there was no one to pick it up and run on.

The fire glowed for a moment, then split asunder and fired the dry sagebrush along the trail. Flames leaped up. Far to the south the Wind Folk saw and knew that someone had stolen from their fire. Angrily they streamed northward, shrieking wildly and carrying with them rain clouds and clouds of dust. Their breath fanned the fire out in all directions, and though they tried first to smother it with dust and then with rain, it burned only the more fiercely.

The frightened fire stealers ran as they had never run before. Mole and Weasel headed underground, and the others tore homeward to raise the alarm. "Up, everyone! Hai! Hurry!" shouted Lone Wolf. "The hills are afire and the Wind Folk are blowing! Up, or you will be roasted in your beds!" Then, as the animal folk milled about in fear and confusion, he gave directions for their safety.

"You antelope, you swift-footed ones—make for the bare rocky mountaintops! You squirrels, you other small folk—into Mole's tunnels and quickly! Hurry or your tails will be singed." But he could think of no safe place for the many animals too large and too slow to flee either up or down until he caught sight of Spider, making haste for a hole in the ground.

"Wait, brother Spider," he cried. "Have you any rope?"

"Yes," said Spider, turning.

"Then get you up and tie it firmly to a piece of the sky." Lone Wolf turned to the others. "We shall roll my lodge over—it will be like a huge tule basket when it is turned upside down and should hold us all." Quickly they tipped the lodge over, and he bade them all climb in, whereupon Spider let down his fine strong rope, and they tied it to the basket.

Coyote had been first to leap into the basket, and the others stretched out beside and atop him. "Come, hurry," he cried, "or we shall be burned to a crisp! I can hear the flames crackling!"

Lone Wolf climbed into the basket last, cried, "Pull away!" and Spider hauled mightily on his rope to hoist them to safety out of reach of the hungry flames. The blaze roared and smoke billowed.

Black Bear, who lay next to Coyote, drawled, "I see you managed to fetch us some hotter fire from the south, friend Coyote." Others grinned, but Coyote pretended not to hear, turning his head to peer out through a small hole in the basket.

"Oh!" he exclaimed. "I can see the ground. I see the fire eating at our sweathouse! If I can tear this hole but a little larger, I shall be able to see how my own house fares. Hai! Already it is but ashes. Tso, tso . . . perhaps if I were to make this hole a mite larger, I should be able to see how fare the folk of my mother's sister's cousin." And with that he picked away, twisting off bits and dropping them through the growing hole.

"Take care," roared Black Bear. "Take care or we shall all fall out of your hole. The basket will burst."

"Nonsense," said Coyote. "Just a bit more and I shall be able to poke my head out. There. Much better. I see Battle Creek and North Mountain . . . and all our land between is ablaze. All is . . . ai! Ai-Aieeee!"

The hole had ripped wider. Clawing frantically, Coyote managed to grasp the torn edge of the basket before he slid through. Hanging from the basket bottom, he cried, "Friend Bear, stretch out your paw and pull me in. I shall surely fall and be roasted!"

Black Bear grinned at the animals who lay beside him and on top of him. "Alas, brother Coyote, we dare not move or the basket will burst asunder. Hold fast! Soon the fire must burn itself out. Hold fast!"

"But my tail will scorch if I dangle here. Pull me up!"

"Tuck it up between your legs," called Mountain Lion in a muffled voice from where he lay beneath Spotted Horse. "We dare not move."

And they did not. When the fire had burned itself out, Spider lowered the basket into the shallows of Battle Creek so that the animals might climb out and cool themselves. They clambered ashore. All except Coyote.

"Come, friend Coyote," all said. "We must find a spot upon which to build a new village. And we will have need of you when the time comes for someone to fetch fire for the first sweathouse ceremony." The laughter spread.

Coyote, scorched and blistered, sat in the water, steaming. "Just go away," he said in dignity. He turned his back.

"Still," said he to himself, "someone *will* have to fetch fire. I might at least be devising a plan for whoever goes. . . ."

The Rescue of Fire

IN the days of rebuilding, the animals gave Coyote no peace. "Aha! Here comes the Scorched One!" they said one to another as he approached. "Ho, Scorcher!" They laughed. "When the smokehouse and sweathouse are built anew, we shall have need of you to raid the Wind Folk once again."

"And so I shall," snapped Coyote. Singed whiskers and a blackened tail had put him in an ill humor. Moreover, fear that the Wind Folk might by now have found a way to protect themselves against future theft left Coyote in doubt of his chances of recovering fire and his own good name.

Yet more ill luck came to plague his thoughts and restless dreams, for word was soon whispered from village to village up through the valleys and ridges of

the land that no longer were the Wind Folk posses-
sors of fire. When mighty Thunder had seen the
flames spreading from the coal Coyote dropped, he
had decided that none but himself was worthy of own-
ing fire. The animals? Clumsy creatures! They laid
waste the land with it. And the Wind Folk? All
bluster! Had they held their breath, had they not
raved so wildly, the land might yet be green. What
matter if the animals could not cook their food or
warm their lodges? What matter if the winds grew
raw and chill? Perchance if all such creatures perished, thought Thunder to himself, he might have
the world to himself, for his own.

So it was that he descended upon the lodge of the
Wind Folk, waving thunderbolts and roaring thun-
derously in a voice that shattered the Wind lodge and
scattered the fearful folk. Once the fire was packed in
straw and wrapped about with green leaves and deer-
hide, Thunder put it under his arm and returned to
his lodge and his daughters—Churning Cloud,
Heavy Rain, Storm Ice, and Swift-as-Lightning. With
them he departed southwards so swiftly and slyly that
no trace of their trail was to be found.

In truth, they had made their way to the Lonely
Mountain. On the crest of its bare and forbidding
heights, they built a new lodge: one with an enor-
mous fire pit and a great gaping smoke hole. To

guard the fire, should they be absent, they paid a small Woswosim bird with bright beads and feathers. Arrayed in this finery, the Woswosim perched in vigilance upon the roof at the smoke-hole's edge; and Thunder knew that no thief could gain entrance. Not for nothing was the Woswosim known as Bird-Who-Never-Sleeps.

Of all this, however, the animals were unaware. Their bones ached with the night cold. With the coming of day, no warm breezes cheered their hearts. Winds were bitter. Noses were cold.

There was no lack of game to eat, but fruits and berries and maize perished in the angry winds. Of the game, only the choicest parts or the most tender kills could be eaten, for it was difficult to chew tough raw meat with chattering teeth. Yet the folk survived despite the selfishness of Thunder.

Some few, indeed, were able to cook their food after a fashion, but such luck was rare. It happened that Eagle owned a bird no larger than a meadow lark, a bird called Toyeskom. Toyeskom was possessed of glaring red eyes so hotly bright that if he were to stare at a haunch of venison for a day and a night, it would become scarcely less tender than if it had been roasted in a bed of coals. But such effort was hard for Toyeskom, and often it was several days before he might sit up once more to stare at a fresh piece of meat. Eagle fared well enough; Lone Wolf was at times his guest; and once Coyote partook of meat in Eagle's lodge, but for the rest he and the villagers chewed wearily at meat that was red and raw.

For warmth at night, all of the folk took to gathering in the new sweathouse; for though no fire burned, it was far warmer to sleep so, packed in closely, than to curl up alone in one's own lodge.

At sunrise those who were not bothered by the chill winds moved outside to sun themselves, to stretch themselves out on the sun-warmed rocks or on the roof of the sweathouse. Thus it was that one morning Lizard and his brother, always the first to rise, in looking south and to the west where the Coast Range disappeared near the southern edge of the world, saw smoke. Thunder's daughters had grown careless. They had fed their morning fire with green wood, and the smoke rose and leveled off, a crooked gray feather. It was enough.

"Smoke! Fire! Smoke!" cried Lizard, tumbling from the roof in his excitement.

"Smoke! Fire! Roast venison!" shrilled Lizard's brother through the smoke hole to the sleeping folk inside.

"Hai! Who? Hei! What?" came the cries of the dazed sleepers. Mouse trilled an alarm on his flute.

"Smoke! Far off at the edge of the sky! Come see

for yourselves!" called Lizard's brother, hopping up and down on the roof.

"Tso, tso," they grumbled, unbelieving. "It is but an angry wind stirring up the dust. Leave us to our sleep."

"Arise!" shouted Lizard at the door. In one hand he held part of his tail, broken off in his fall; with the other he beckoned eagerly. "Stir yourselves! You can see the plume of smoke with your own eyes if you will but stir."

"Tso, tso." They laughed. "It is a foolish lizard who does not know a dust spirit when he sees it. Leave us to our rest."

The excited Lizard climbed back to the roof to look once more. "It *is* smoke," he cried. "Oh, come!" There was no answer but laughter.

Coyote, thinking to make the animals laugh yet louder, crept to the doorway to scoop up a pawful of dust. When next Lizard's brother called, "Good folk, arise and see!" Coyote threw the dust onto the roof. "Dust spirits! Only dust spirits!" He laughed as the two lizards coughed and spluttered, rubbing the grit from their eyes. The folk inside would have laughed again had not Lone Wolf arisen to speak his mind.

"It is ill, Coyote, that such an important fellow as yourself should torment folk. Do you feel the wiser for making others seem foolish? Do you feel the stronger for making others suffer? Better it were for you to say to us, 'Come, my people. Our brothers the lizards have seen a feather of smoke, and together we will look to see if it be truly so.' "

The other folk were ashamed as well, for their laughter had encouraged Coyote's taunt. They arose and went out, and a downcast Coyote held his tongue and followed. Upon being asked where the smoke was to be seen, the lizards pointed it out eagerly so that all might see its thin smudge trailing up and across the faraway sky.

"It is true!" breathed Spotted Horse.

"We should not have laughed," nodded Black Bear. "We have lost precious time."

Lizard agreed. "If Thunder awakens while it yet smokes, he may move his lodge again. To rescue the fire, we must move swiftly."

"But how shall we rescue it?" ventured another. "Thunder is strong and we are but puny."

"Yes," chimed in others. "If we anger him, he will cut us down like grass. How are we to rescue the fire without grave danger?"

And one said timidly, "It is not all that unpleasant to chew uncooked meat." Others might have echoed him had not Eagle appeared in the door of his own lodge to command their attention.

"The bravest," said Eagle, "must lead the search

for Thunder's lodges. We must have fire. Winter is yet to come. We will have need of it; and even though Thunder is strong, though he is wicked, we must try. When we find him, some one of us will think of a way to outwit him. But we must waste no more time."

"Eagle speaks with wisdom," said Coyote, moving forward. "And but for me, we should have been off sooner. Come, let us go."

Southward and to the west raced the animals. Squirrel, Mole, and many of the smaller folk soon fell behind, but Mouse rode clinging to the back of Swaia the deer, who was not far behind Coyote and Dog. So eager had Mouse been that he still carried his flute.

For many hours they traveled so, until it could be seen that the smoke arose from the top of the Lonely Mountain. Confused, the animals stopped to argue what should be done. Eagle, as before, spoke wisely; and so it happened that Mouse, Dog, Deer, and Coyote were chosen to climb the mountain.

They were several hours about it. When at last they were a short distance below Thunder's lodge, they halted for a brief war council. In the midst of their planning, the sound of a song came down to them: the song of Woswosim, who crooned, "I am

Bird-Who-Never-Sleeps. Here am I . . . Bird-Who-Never-Sleeps." He sat atop Thunder's lodge by the smoke hole and sang.

"What chance have we to pass a Bird-Who-Never-Sleeps?" said Swaia to Dog and Coyote and Mouse. But Mouse calmed their fears. He alone, small as he was, might creep past the watching Woswosim. From pebble to pebble he crept upwards, while his companions scarce dared to breathe. Along the trail, up a dangling rawhide cord, to the roof's edge he went. Still Woswosim sang, "I am the Bird-Who-Never-Sleeps."

But it was not so. Mouse could clearly see that Woswosim's eyes were closed, that Bird-Who-Never-Sleeps was asleep in spite of the song he crooned. Carefully Mouse crept to the smoke-hole's edge. Below, the oak fire had burned down to coals. No smoke arose. Four women slept in a circle around the fire, head to toe. Thunder was not to be seen. Swiftly Mouse shinned down a lodge pole, stole close, and chewed neatly through the waist string of Churning Cloud's apron skirt of rushes. Then he moved on, doing the same with Heavy Rain, Storm Ice, and Swift-as-Lightning, so that they might be delayed if the alarm was raised too soon.

That done, Mouse filled his flute with coals from the fire. Then quickly he ran to rejoin his companions below. There they divided the fire, for Thunder surely could not catch them all. One coal was wrapped thickly in green leaves and put in Dog's ear, whereupon he dashed downhill and away. Coyote, wiser than before in the ways of fire, took between his teeth a piece wrapped in the same way and set off at once. Mouse and his flute, warm with the last coals, rode upon swift Swaia's back. Only silence followed them, and all seemed well.

All was well—for a while. The companions were nearing the spot where they had left their fellow villagers when Thunder's voice roared out. Something had brought him back: the dying fire or perhaps the smell of stranger.

"What has happened to my fire?" he thundered. Into the lodge he raged, tumbling his daughters from their dreams. "Someone has stolen from my fire!" roared he.

Up leaped his daughters. Down fell their apron skirts. Hastily they sat down and drew the aprons up to tie them on again with fumbling fingers. "Hasten!" fumed Thunder.

"Where? Who? How? What?" babbled his daughters. Apron skirts secure, they streamed after Thunder, who thudded down the mountainside, booming furiously.

The animals heard and saw the wild lightning

forks, the torrents of hail and swirling rain clouds that his daughters bore with them.

"Run!" screamed Spotted Horse.

"Run!" shrilled Squirrel.

"Run!" croaked Coyote as he ran. And as he spoke, his coal dropped and rolled away, to be scooped up by Heavy Rain, who was close upon his heels.

"Tso, tso!" Dog laughed breathlessly. "Coyote has dropped his fire again!" And he sped on, shaking his head and laughing. Scarcely had he gone half a mile when, still shaking his head, he felt the coal fall from his ear to the ground. Before he could stop, Churning Cloud had swooped down to snatch it up. There was no fire left but that of Mouse.

"Friend Mouse, I can run no farther," panted Swaia. "Pass the fire to one who has not run so far."

First Panther ran with the flute, and then Fox. Tree Squirrel took it, leading Thunder and his daughters a wild chase up tree and down tree. Then Ground Squirrel caught up the fire and bore it along, in and out of many tunnels in the earth. When at last he neared Clear Lake, he was wearied beyond running, and he passed the flute to Frog. But Frog could not leap swiftly enough to elude Thunder and Storm Ice.

They grasped him by the tail just as he leaped for the safety of a rock beyond the water's edge. It tore

completely off. Storm Ice was left with it in her hand, and it is for this that frogs have never since kept their tails.

The flute flew through the air and came to rest atop a hollow stump nearby. Thunder reached out with a roar. "My fire! My fire is mine once more!"

Too soon did he speak, for in the hollow stump lived Skunk, and Skunk feared no one. Stepping angrily from his door, he shot at Thunder, wounding him. Churning Cloud, Heavy Rain, Storm Ice, and Swift-as-Lightning rushed to their father, wailing for fear he was dead.

"How dare you come about here meddling with decent folk?" fumed Skunk. "Have you no home? Hei? Then go there and leave us in peace, for if I see you about again, I shall not shoot so gently."

Because of his words the four women, now silent, carried their father Thunder off to the Lonely Mountain top. No longer do they walk the earth; but when they fight among themselves, hailstones and lightning forks and torrents of water are thrown across the sky; and the voice of Thunder is still heard.

Mouse, of course, retrieved his flute, returning safely home with his people. And folk have had fire ever since.

Coyote's New Hairdo

SAPSUCKER was quite a handsome fellow. Bright red were the feathers of his head and breast, and he knew well how to comb them and how to dress himself so that he might look the most elegant of birds. Twice daily he bathed in fresh running water, whether he were in the mountains or wintering near the ocean coast. He took to combing his head feathers new ways so that he might stand out among other birds of his own kind. It seemed to the other folk that if Sapsucker were not out parading up and down, he was in his lodge making new head nets.

Coyote envied Sapsucker his good looks. "Who but my wife ever looks at me?" thought he. "If only I had such beautiful red hair! What a handsome dog *I* should be!" Hopefully, he tried the juices of red berries, but they only stained his fur with patches of purple and brown. "If only I could make my hair stand up in such a crest as his!" wished Coyote. He combed it up, but down it fell, as smooth as ever. He tied it up with a thong, but the hair slipped out from the knot. He dampened it with water and shaped it upwards, but when the water dried, his hair stood out in all directions. At last, in desperation, he sought Sapsucker's help. He must have a head net.

"How do you make such *bolmaki,* such head nets? Of what do you make the string? It seems so fine and the weaving so delicate. Of course," Coyote added, "I know that you laugh at my ill luck as do the others. Everyone teases me, lies to me, so that they may trick me and laugh at my foolishness. But about this head net I am serious, and I trust you will tell me the truth. My heart is set on having such a hairdo as yours. It would please me to look as sleek as you."

"Why, thank you, brother Coyote," said Sapsucker in surprise. "But I would not think of lying to you. Your hair should do quite well with a smooth, high crest. Since your hair is not red and I do not have large ears, no one is likely to confuse the two of us— and I could have no other reason than that to deny you. No, I shall be glad to see you try a head net such as mine. It is really quite a simple thing."

"Look," said he. "To make string so fine as this, I

use *kololo*. For fiber, you scrape this outer part and use it just as do the fishermen when they make string nets from milkweed fiber. When it is well mixed and mashed, you must spread it upon a rock at the fire's edge and leave it until it be dry as bone. The twining and twisting of it into string is easy, and once it is spliced so that you have four good pieces of a length about—well, about ten or fifteen times the length of your arm—then you are ready to weave. See—here is one half finished. To put it on your head takes a bit of practice. I comb my hair to a peak, so. Then with a bit of water I wet it and smooth the peak forward. On slips the head net, in slips the hair skewer, and all is fastened neatly and tightly for the day."

"Hah!" snorted Coyote. "It is as I thought. You do not tell me the truth for fear I shall look more handsome than you. It is impossible to slip such a net over wet hair without smashing it flat. It cannot be done. Come now, Sapsucker, tell me the truth, for I am not one to be easily fooled."

Sapsucker shook his head. "I tell you, brother, that *is* the way it is done!"

"Well, I do not believe it. Tell me once more—and this time, the truth!"

Again Sapsucker described the making of the head net and the way in which he put it on. Again Coyote insisted that such was not the truth. "It cannot be," said he. "You shook your head, and your hairdo never quivered. Not a hair moved from place. There is some secret way of combing, some way of stiffening, that you hide from me."

Sapsucker sighed. He knew argument to be useless. Coyote would hang about and bother him all day. "Very well," said he, thinking quickly, "since you do not believe what I have told you, I shall tell you the truth of it. You are a hard one to fool, Coyote. But if you will promise to tell no other creature, I shall share my secret with you."

"Yes, yes! Of course." Coyote's whiskers twitched eagerly.

"First of all, in the heat of the day I seek in the forest for a sugar-pine tree that drips much gum from a broken branch or some such wound, and this gum I gather on a large piece of pine bark. You must have quite a bit, if all is to go well. When I have enough, I mix into it a fine dust, stirring it up with a hair skewer, adding more dust until there is a thick ball of it, much like the pitch cakes we make for starting the sweathouse fire."

"Hai, I see!" Coyote grinned. "It is *that* you use instead of water!"

"Yes, but first you must comb your hair and tie it up so that you have the right shape."

"So! That sounds much better. Many thanks, good

Sapsucker. How fine I shall look!" said Coyote. "I shall search out the kololo now, and on the morrow I shall find a sappy tree." And so he did. The head net he wove, the dust he sifted, and the mixture he mixed. When all was ready, he trotted off to Battle Creek, found his favorite pool, and sat down to peer at himself in the water. Carefully he combed his hair and tied it up with a bit of string. With the long, sharp hair skewer, he dipped up a bead of the pitch and spread it upon his hair. It was hard to spread smoothly. After another daub or two he thought, "Ai! It will take forever to do a drop at a time."

Being eager to finish, to stroll to the sweathouse while the animals had not yet gone in, he dipped his paws in the pitch and smeared it upwards over the crest of his hair. The string slipped off and stuck fast to one paw, but his hair stayed in place. Into the water he looked, admiringly. The pointed crest looked rather like a third ear atop his head, but it was really quite handsome, he thought. "But I hardly think I need the hairnet after all," said he to himself. "My hair holds firmly as it is. And since my fur is much the color of dust, it looks quite right without a net." Quickly he rubbed his paws in dry dust and then together to remove the pitch. Then he hurried home, hung his softest and best rabbit-skin robe across his shoulders, and headed toward the sweathouse for the daily sweat bath and cold plunge that his people loved so well.

"Tso, tso! Look who comes yonder," cried the folk.

"Coyote? Can that handsome fellow be Coyote?" said one.

"Why are you so richly decked out, friend Coyote?"

Yet another said, laughing, "It would seem that he wishes to charm the daughters of Sapsucker. They would admire one such as he. What says your wife of it, Coyote?"

But altogether they were greatly impressed. While the fire tender built up the fire to heat the air inside the sweathouse, the folk outside complimented the parading Coyote in flattering words. Then they said, "Why do we not honor Coyote today? We shall have a fanning contest, and as he feels so fine today, he shall be first to be fanned." Coyote was greatly pleased and confident that he could stand the rushing hot air as long as any of them. It was, after all, an honor to be first.

So it was agreed. When the fire tender called, Coyote entered by the east door and stood by the fire. From the west the others entered and took up the large deerskin fans that stood by the door. From across the fire they fanned Coyote, swirling the heated air around him until the sweathouse was an oven, until the air he breathed seemed made of burning needles. Sweating heavily, panting harshly, at last he moved away and stretched out in his usual spot by the wall. Merrily the fanners followed, circling the fire and fanning wildly.

"So it is a game you play!" Coyote laughed. "Then I shall play it too!"

He snatched up a fan and the battle was joined. Back and forth and around they staggered in the heat —two times, three times around. Outside, their womenfolk worried, for the whole of the sweathouse roof was leaking smoke as if it were about to leap into flame at any moment. As they watched, Mink appeared in the western doorway, dropped his fan, and dashed in the direction of the creek. Sizzling, he sank into the chilly water. "They will all be ill from such foolishness!" mourned their wives.

Four times had the fanners forced Coyote back when the pitch began to melt. A drop fell upon his shoulder. "Tso!" he shrilled. "Aiee!" and his companions thought he screamed from fear of the heat.

"Why, this is nothing," they joked. "The fires are not so hot as they were in our youth!" And they fanned all the harder.

The pitch dripped down Coyote's nose and onto his chest. "Ai, ai, aieee!" cried he as it began to burn.

His head ablaze, he tore through the door and
headed for the water. Pups and kits and other youngsters playing in the village saw him streak by. The
womenfolk were struck silent with amazement, but
the children loudly cried out the alarm. "Old Coyote
is burning up, burning up! Old Man Coyote's topknot is afire! Come see, come see!" they cried as they
followed fast upon his heels. The wives and other villagers were not far behind. Blazing like a torch, Coyote led them to the creek.

Head first he hurtled in. The fire was quenched.
But the damage had been done. Gone was his topknot, bare was his pate. As bare it was as if he had
been scalped. The villagers stood and stared. Coyote
sat and glared.

"Coyote, Coyote!" cried his wife, pushing to the
front of the crowd. "Can you never cease trying new
ways to get yourself into trouble? Look at you! Bald
as an egg!"

The menfolk were politely silent, but the other
womenfolk laughed. One asked of Coyote's wife,
"Why is it that no one else was scorched? Why only
Coyote?"

Coyote's wife had spoken with Sapsucker, and so
she could tell the tale of the pitch on his hair. "Never
have I heard of such a foolish thing," said she in dis-

gust. Whereupon she took him by the arm, helped him home, put him to bed, covered him well, hushed his groans, and sang him to sleep.

"Hei, hai!" She sighed. "That is my Coyote!"

The Witsduks

ITSDUK" means "Snow the Wind Blows and Drifts," and once an old woman of that name caused much grief in this world. She, with her family and folk, took great joy in tormenting all whom they met. They were small, ill-tempered, and thought nothing more delightful than to see Swaia shiver; to fly at the eyes of Mountain Lion to blind him; or to take away the breath of Spotted Horse. Eagle and his folk at length tired of huddling over lodge fires, of shaking the clinging Witsduks from eyelashes or whiskers.

"Will not someone rid us of these creatures?" asked the folk of Eagle's village.

"Will not someone rid us of these creatures?" complained each one to another. Cutuk, the rock squirrel, listened as the question went its rounds and thought. Her wisdom was great, for she was old and a medicine woman; and her courage was no less than her wisdom. One thing alone gave her doubt, and of this at last she spoke.

"I am old," she said, "and in the pouch of my memory I hold magic, a medicine with which to trick, to trap such mean folk as old Witsduk and her family. Willingly would I destroy them, but I fear Wus, the fox. He is a tease and you may laugh at his tricks, but his teasing is evil. To put the Witsduks in my sack is one feat, but to slip past Wus is a greater. He would laugh to loose them: to snatch the sack, to untie it, and to set the Witsduks upon us."

"He must not! He shall not!" cried the animals, eager to see Cutuk on her way to the mountain where their tormentors lived. "We will stop him," they said.

Eagle nodded. "Good, my people. Wus is likely off upon some mischief now; I know not where. Some score of you must follow Cutuk. If friend Wus appears, you must stop him any way you can. Our old folk and our children cannot much longer stand the harshness of the Witsduks. Wus must not meddle in this."

"He shall not!" answered a score of the bravest.

From her lodge Cutuk brought a large sack tightly woven from tough grasses. She carried it folded under her arm. Into the beaded pouch at her belt, she had put a long buckskin thong, her head strap for carrying burdens, a pair of mittens, and a fur hood. With the bravest of Eagle's people at her back, she set out for the white-topped mountain where lived Witsduk's people. At the mountain's foot, her followers halted to keep watch upon the trail. Cutuk hobbled on.

Not far below the crest, she crept among the rocks to hide. Her sack she opened, spreading wide its mouth. For a long while she crouched low, waiting, silent. Above, atop the ridge, the Witsduks rushed about and around: some in a whirling dance, some shrieking and chattering shrilly into the wind. Old Cutuk wore her mittens and hood but was fast becoming frozen. When at last they came near to her hiding place, her frozen paws could scarce hold the gaping sack. None saw her. As they passed by, Cutuk softly said words of medicine, of magic.

Into the bag danced the Witsduks. They could not stop themselves. More streamed down into the rocks where Cutuk chanted the words that none but she knew. Into the sack they rushed, and she pushed, crowded, and shoved them in more tightly yet. The last in, the sack full, she fumbled in her pouch for the buckskin thong, whipped it about the neck of the sack, and tied it with stout knots. The carrying strap

she fastened securely and slipped its headband into
place over her forehead. Sack upon her back, she
stumbled numbly down the trail.

The air grew warmer. Her feet grew more sure. At
the foot of the mountain, she hailed those who
waited. "Hai, good folk! In my sack every Witsduk in
the world is packed! Come follow to the deepest of
canyons, where I shall bury the sack under a flood of
sliding stones. And keep watch for Wus! I fear him
yet."

"But there has been no sign of him, Old One."

"Yet I fear to meet him. He would give me no
peace. Were he to open my sack, no creature would
be safe. It is for this I fear. The anger of the Witsduks would spill over the land, bringing cold death
—and never could they be trapped or tricked again.
You must come with me."

The animals said, "Oh yes, Old Cutuk. If Wus
comes our way, we shall stop him. We could sit upon
his head . . . or tie him up . . . or . . ." But the
thought of the spiteful anger of Wus dismayed them.
What if they should have to kill old Wus? For a while
unhappily they followed Cutuk, then one by one they
turned back.

Alone Cutuk kept on until a great log fallen across
the trail gave her pause. Pushing the sack up first, she
climbed atop the log and saw Wus. He was crouched

below her, reaching with one paw under the log and calling in a sweet voice, "Here Mouse, little Mouse. Come out and talk to your brother Wus." Cutuk did not move. What was best to do? Perhaps he would pay no attention to her if he were hunting. If she tiptoed to the end of the log, he might not catch sight of her before she gained cover in the chinquapin bushes there. Cautiously she moved.

"Hai, grandmother! Where might you be tiptoeing with such a bulging sack? One might think you did not want Wus to see you!"

Nervously the old squirrel laughed. "Oh no, good Wus. It was that I had no wish to disturb your mouse hunt."

"You are kind, grandmother." Wus smiled, showing his teeth. "But the mouse is gone. What have you in your sack? Where are you going? If that be food, in kindness you should give me some as I have lost the mouse."

"No, no. It is not food."

"I am not so sure. You would not speak with a double tongue, my grandmother? No, no, Cutuk is honest. Good honest Cutuk, you must let me help you down from this log so that you may be on your way. Here, I will lift down the sack. You are too old for such a heavy load."

"No. It is not heavy. I will manage," she insisted,

lifting the sack easily in her hands and slinging it across her back again. The head band she fitted across her forehead once more.

"So full and yet so light?" Wus threw up his paws as if astonished. "What do you carry? It is milkweed pods! You are going to dry and scrape them and make string from their insides. Open the sack that I may see! My bow needs a new string, and I know not which pods are best to gather. Open the sack that I may see."

"I have no milkweed pods," said Cutuk, edging away.

"Then it *must* be food. Some new food." Wus teased. "Wus loves to try new foods. Kind grandmother, do untie your sack and give me a taste."

"You would not like the taste of these."

Wus moved along the log beside her. "Ah, so you have tasted them?"

There was no escaping him. At last Cutuk sighed. "In this sack I carry nothing new. They are creatures you hate as much as I. Many times they have made your teeth chatter and your breath to become ice in the air. I go to bury them forever, to rid the world of them."

"Give them to me," said Wus. "I shall eat them here and save you carrying them further. There is nothing under the sun and moon I cannot eat, whether it crawls or walks or flies. Wind and air I can eat; rain and clouds are tasty to me. You can have nothing in your burden sack that is not food for Wus. Wus can eat everything!"

"You are not fooling? You can eat any folk that walk this world?" asked Cutuk.

"Any. Try me. There is nothing I cannot eat."

"What of the Witsduks? It is the Witsduks I carry in my sack. Surely you do not wish to eat such as they?"

Wus swallowed uncomfortably but insisted that he was eager to feast upon Witsduk. Cutuk leaped from the log and tried to push past the stubborn fox. No good could come of arguing with such a one. But Wus was not to be ignored. From behind he grabbed her head strap angrily and pulled. It cut at her forehead, and as old Cutuk stumbled backwards, she knew that she was beaten.

"Very well, foolish one. Take the sack," she said. She unfastened the strap from her burden. "Take it, untie it, and eat them if you will. But wait at least until I have crossed the flatland and am well away!" She turned and ran.

Her old legs carried her as swiftly as if they had been young. But fast as she was, Wus had loosened the buckskin string before she reached the middle of the flat.

Out slipped the first Witsduks. One by one they came, and the greedy fox caught and ate each one. When Cutuk had almost reached the far edge of the plain, he loosened the string yet more. Angry Witsduks poured from the mouth of the sack and spilled upon the ground. Wus had hard work to catch them all. He dashed about, snapping his jaws in all directions, gobbled as fast as he could, ate them all; ate and ate until he could eat no more.

He did not think to tie the sack again. The Witsduks inside milled about, beating at its walls, pushing toward its mouth. The string slipped to the ground, the mouth gaped wide, and out rushed the Witsduks in a great crowd. Furious, they ran in all directions. Wus was at last frightened. He turned tail and fled.

Old Woman Witsduk followed him, shrieking, "Tso, tso! You would trick my people into a sack, would you? You would eat my children's children, would you? I'll pinch your nose for that!"

The other Witsduks streamed behind her, shrilling, "I'll chatter his teeth, I will! Let me pass— I'll frost his toes! I'll freeze his knees, I will, I will!" They overtook and surrounded him. Wus beat at them, brushed them from his eyes, and barked for help. They swarmed. They flurried. They pinched

and prodded. When they left him for dead at the side
of the trail, he looked like a frosted snow fox, stiff
legs in the air. From his mouth out came the hordes
of Witsduks he had eaten. None were hurt, and all
were angrier than Old Woman Witsduk and their
brothers had been.

In a cloud they swept about the land, seeking creatures to torment, to chill, to kill. Many small folk,
caught unawares, were frozen in their tracks. Cutuk
had reached the safety of her home in the rocks, and
most of Eagle's villagers had crowded into their warm
smokehouse—except for those who in their fear of
Wus had left old Cutuk to go on alone. Those cow-
ered in their own lodges in shame.

The Witsduks live to this day and will live forever,
roving from place to place. Only Cutuk had the
magic to trap them, and, once tried, it would never
work again. The animals learned to grow thick,
shaggy coats for the season when the Witsduks were
about. Black Bear and Little Brown Bear took to
sleeping the cold season away, snug in their caves. No
one yet can live at the place where Wus opened the
sack—one would freeze or starve, for Old Woman
Witsduk lives there still.

When the worst was over, Coyote rescued Wus and

thawed him out, but never was he quite the same as before. White-haired and suspicious he was. And snow foxes—the Arctic foxes of the North—still speak of him as their Grandfather Wus.

Coyote and Mole

THE day was bright, the sky clear, the breeze cool—too fine a day to lie abed. Coyote stretched, scratched, and shook himself, and set his feet upon the trail. No thought had he which way his feet should take him. On such a day any road to anywhere would do. Too fine a day it was to worry, to work, to fish or hunt. Sweet was the breeze. Happily sniffing, nose in the air, Coyote jogged along. And tripped.

Mole had been digging a hole. Feet clawing the air, he lay sprawled upon his back, and Coyote was stretched flat a few feet beyond. "Hei, hai!" Coyote laughed. "Hello, cousin! Why do you work in the middle of the road in the middle of a day made only for play?"

Mole snorted and scrambled to his feet. Carefully

he dusted his fur, strode to his hole, picked up a small sack, and walked away, muttering, "Very well, I shall dig elsewhere. But folk might think to look where they put their feet!"

"Tso, tso!" exclaimed Coyote, catching hold of Mole's stubby tail. "Where do you go so fast, Old Grumble? Is it kind to cause such a crash and then go off without offering a fellow a bit of your tobacco? My pipe is empty and your pouch is full. Come— just enough for one smoke!"

"I have no tobacco, and I would thank you, Coyote, to loose me."

Coyote shook his head in answer. "Come now, cousin. Your bag is bulging with tobacco, more than a small fellow like yourself has need for."

Mole clutched the top of the bag more carefully and repeated, "I have no tobacco. There is none in my sack. I have spoken truth. Now loose my tail!"

"Very well. As soon as I have seen in your sack."

"No! It holds nothing of interest to you."

"I am always interested in tobacco." Coyote teased.

"Hai! I tell you I have no tobacco weed!"

"Show me."

"No."

"Well then. If you must be so stubborn, I fear that I shall have to take it and look for myself." He

snatched the sack and, as he untied it, up the road
flashed Mole, his short legs scrambling.

The sack was full of fleas. Coyote yelped and
hopped and shook and shrilled, "Come back, cousin
Mole! Take back your sack!" But Mole was safely far
away, snug in his own home hole.

It was that day that Coyote learned to howl his
famous howl.

Cottontail's Song

ne fine June morning Cottontail lay in the shade of a wild rosebush where he had sought refuge from the scorching sun. It was a choice siesta spot, and Cottontail contentedly stretched out upon his back to scratch his stomach. And all the while he sang a song.

It happened that Coyote, even though the noonday sun was high and fierce, was at the time walking across the desert; and thus it was that the song came to his ears. He pricked them up, paused, and listened. The voice was familiar. He looked around. "Ho, Brother Cottontail," he called. "Where are you?"

The song stopped. In the middle of a word it came to an end. Puzzled, Coyote called again. "Brother, where are you? That was a very pretty song you sang.

I have never heard a better. It would be good if I had
such a song to sing by the sweathouse fire. I would be
much pleased to learn it."

From his shelter on the foothill just above, Cottontail shouted his answer: "No! It is my song and so it
will stay. You cannot have it."

"Just once. Sing it for me just once," said Coyote,
trotting toward the spot where he thought the voice
had come from.

"No. I shall not sing it again, not even once. It
belongs to me, and I do not see why I should give it
to you. It is mine. Go away!"

Coyote paused to ponder. "Such a pretty song! I
need just such a song to sing as I trot along. It would
make traveling a pleasure. Dear brother," he called
aloud. "Your heart is good. How can you refuse me
so cruelly? If you sing it once more, I shall be
satisfied."

Not wishing to be thought cruel or meanly selfish,
Cottontail sighed. "Hei, hai! Well, if it is but
once . . ." and he sang the song through from its beginning to its end. Coyote, his ears cocked, nodded in
time to the time.

"Now I know it!" He laughed to himself, and,
"Thanks, many thanks, good brother," called he to
Cottontail. Then as he had been on his way to the
spring beyond Black Rock before he heard the song,

he set off again in that direction, singing as he jogged along, stepping to the rhythm of the tune. One verse, two verses, three verses . . . but there, halfway, he found he could go no further. The rest he had forgotten. He tried beginning once more at the beginning. It was of no use. "Hai," he thought. "What a pity! I shall have to see whether Cottontail will not sing it for me again." And so he turned back toward the foothills.

"No!" answered Cottontail angrily. "I said once only. I meant once only. I sang it once. That will have to do you. Good afternoon. Good-by."

"Oh, oh, oh! Hei, hai, how did it go? How did it go?" Coyote fretted, running about in a circle.

"You should not have forgotten it," called Cottontail.

"It would not happen again," pleaded Coyote. "Sing it for me this once, and I shall not bother you again. I shall hold fast to every word."

"Oh, well." Cottontail sighed, thinking to be rid of him. "Just this once; no more. Mind you, now. This is the last time." Whereupon he sang his song again.

Coyote nodded thoughtfully and wagged his tail in time with the tune. Then, after thanking Cottontail, he was off once more at a brisk jog-trot, singing happily. It was a marvelously good song, and he rolled the words off his tongue with great gusto. One

verse, two. . . . No, that was not the right word. How did the second verse begin? Yes, that was right, but he could not get past the middle of it. He had lost half of what he had remembered the first time. He turned back.

Cottontail, humming softly and sunning himself contentedly, was startled by the appearance of Coyote's nose among the roses. "Dear brother." Coyote smiled. "A portion of the song has slipped my mind again, and I should count it a kind favor if you would sing it through once more."

"No," answered Cottontail firmly. "I cannot. I will not." He closed his eyes.

"Not once more, dear brother? You know that I will not forget it again. Surely your heart is not so hard as flint? Surely it will soften long enough for you to sing the song once more?"

Cottontail shook his head. "Your chance is past. You took it, and a second chance as well. You cannot have a third."

"Very well," said Coyote, thinking quickly. "I shall have to earn a third chance. What do you say about a contest? We shall have a contest to find out who wins the song." Cottontail opened one eye as Coyote continued, "Yes, the one with the strongest lungs should win the song. That is only fair. We will find a place where rocks are piled like an oven, and we shall build a fire in front of the opening in the rocks. The one who can sit inside in the heat and smoke for the longest time wins the song."

Never one to decline a contest, Cottontail agreed. "Very well," he said. "Find such a place and I will be willing."

About a mile farther into the foothills, Coyote sighted a rock with a large cavelike hole under one side, and with Cottontail's help he built a roaring fire before the opening. "There!" he exclaimed, dusting off his paws. "That should do. Now I shall go first, as is only fair, this being my idea. After I have stayed for as long as my lungs and eyes can stand the heat and smoke, you shall have your turn. The song shall go to the stronger of us. I have spoken!"

His eyes twinkling, Cottontail nodded in agreement. Silently he waited, feeding wood into the fire until after a short time Coyote stumbled out, gasping for air, his eyes red and streaming. "Whoo! Hai!" He coughed. "How terrible it is in there! One can scarcely breathe. Surely you shall do better than I."

As Cottontail slipped behind the fire without a word, Coyote shook his head sadly. "He is a game little fellow. Such a pity that he is so small! He cannot stand it in there for more than a moment or two at best. The heat is bad, but the smoke is worse." He rubbed his own reddened eyes.

A moment passed. And another. "Now he will come out." Coyote smiled. But there was no sound from behind the crackling fire. He waited. He paced up and down. Cottontail did not appear. After a much longer wait, Coyote sighed. "Ai, poor thing! The smoke has been too much for him. He is certainly dead and half roasted by now. What a pity!" He shrugged and turned to make his way back to the desert floor.

After a time, with Coyote well out of earshot, Cottontail came around from his hiding place behind the rock. Coyote, being much larger, had not noticed the small hole at the back of the rock hollow.

Stretching out in the sunshine, Cottontail smiled and sang his song.

The Out-Foxed Fox

Gray Wolf, who lived alone outside of Eagle's village, had been ill for a long while. Because few of the animals passed by his lodge, no one knew of his illness until Wus stopped by one day. "Perhaps he has left a bit of meaty bone or nice liver lying about," thought Wus as he peered into the dark doorway. He was startled to see a pile of blankets move and Gray Wolf's nose poke out from under them.

"Why, friend Wolf!" he stammered in confusion. "I h-had thought you were . . . were off on a hunt . . ."

Gray Wolf waved a weak paw. "Ah, brother Wus . . . good Fox. I have been very sick, too sick to leave my bed. I have had no food in a week. Please, good Wus—bring me something to eat, for I am dying of hunger."

Wus was shocked to see how poorly old Gray Wolf appeared but saw at once a chance to put the big fellow in his debt. For favors done, one might with justice expect a haunch or two of venison. He went outdoors, sniffed along the ground, and soon returned with several mice, which he put upon a wooden plate and offered to Gray Wolf. They were gone in one bite. "Ah, that is better." Gray Wolf sighed. "It is only that I am so weak. My paws shake and my whiskers twitch. It is real meat that I need: good red meat."

"Well," pondered Wus. "I know of a few good rabbit holes."

"No, I am *hungry!* You must find me deer: good venison."

"I? But I have never hunted anything so large or so fast in my life!"

"Well then, you must trick them into coming here. Let me see. . . . If you tell them that I am dying and that you are having a great dance to celebrate it, they would surely come. When you have them in here where they cannot run, you can choose a fat white-faced one and kill it."

Wus was doubtful but set out to try his cunning. Up the trail toward the mountain he trotted, calling,

"Ho, Deer! Ho, you mountain folk! Come dance, come dance with me, for Gray Wolf, old Big-Ribs, is sick to death and—hei, hai—I am glad!" Wus's shout of glee was quite convincing. But at first there was no answer.

"Ho, Deer! Hai, Deer! Old Big-Ribs is dying. The gray shadow who has eaten so many of your friends and children is dying! Come dance with me around the one who has hounded and hunted you all these years. Come dance with me!"

High on the ridge Big Deer heard and laughed. "Come, my people! Do you hear? Gray Wolf is dying, and Wus calls us to join in the death dance. Let us go down and dance!"

As they bounded down the mountain trail, Wus ran to tell Gray Wolf. "They come," said he. "It worked!"

Gray Wolf stretched out upon his bed, and Wus covered him from ears to toes with skins. When a great number of deer had wedged into the lodge, Wus began the death dance. He took a club with which to beat at the death spirits, and several times as he danced past Gray Wolf's still form, Wus forgot to pretend and let fly a solid whack. As he chanted and skipped and shuffled, the deer followed behind, raising a great dust that filled the lodge and set all to coughing and weeping.

"Enough! Enough!" cried Big Deer. "Gray Wolf must be dead by now. If he is not, he should be—and soon we will all smother from the dust. Let us be on our way, for we must be home by dusk. And thank you, brother Wus, for asking us to dance with you."

"Very well," said Wus. "And if he is not dead by morning, I shall call you that we may try again."

The first to leave were the white-faced deer. They towered so high over Wus, their hooves were so sharp and their antlers so many-pronged, that he feared to even touch them. The last to leave was a fawn whom Wus held back with a question as to whether grass was good to eat. When the older deer were out of sight, Wus set upon the young one and killed it.

"Very good. Tender and sweet." Gray Wolf nodded, sitting up after finishing the roast fawn. "And done to a turn. But I need more than such a lean mouthful as that—much more. Why did you not kill a good fat white-face as I told you?"

Wus was offended. "They slipped past me in the dust," said he. "Besides, there was no room to jump at them or swing the club in that crowd. I cannot kill a deer by snapping at his ankles."

Gray Wolf lay back weakly. "I suppose not. Do not call them back tomorrow, but call the Wuyus, the mountain sheep, instead. They love me no better than do the deer, and perhaps you will find them easier game."

On the morning following, Wus went out and called, "O nimble-footed rock climbers, fleecy Wuyus, come dance! I dance for the death of Gray Wolf, he who lurked and leaped and gave you chase and killed so many of your flock. He dies today, and I am glad! Come dance! I dance because of his greed. Never when he killed deer did he give me a bite, so I am glad. Come dance!"

When Wus saw the first of the big-horned mountain sheep come toward the lodge, he wrapped Gray Wolf as before. Gray Wolf whispered, "When the dance is over, find a full-grown ewe. Their flesh is firm and tender."

The sheep poured in, bleating and laughing. Again Wus took up his club and began the dance, beating the "death spirits" into the well-wrapped wolf. For a long while the sheep danced wildly and stirred up a choking dust. When the time of their leaving came, the mighty horns of the rams and the great width of the ewes left Wus fearful, and they went past him one by one until he saw that a puny young ram was last. "Stay a moment," said Wus. "The door is narrow, and such a small fellow as you could well be trampled."

Before very long, Gray Wolf sat up to the meal Wus had prepared. His paws still trembled and he could not stand, and so Wus fed him once more. "Tso," said Gray Wolf. "My belly is not so empty now, but it is far from full. Such soft and mushy meat is never filling. I shall never get my strength back on such fare as this. Something that is fat and prime. That is what I need."

Wus sighed. "I have done my best. If you were well enough to lend a hand, I might do better, but . . ."

Gray Wolf agreed to try, and Wus jogged off to call the antelopes, who also had many a good reason to be glad of the death of Big-Ribs. When Wus saw that they had heard and were coming to join him in his dance, he returned to tell the wolf.

"Take a larger club," said Gray Wolf, "and cover me with only a thin grass mat. And keep the dust down so that I may see." Wus nodded and, going out of doors, sang of the greed of Big-Ribs, who always drove him away when there was meat to eat. When all of the antelopes had followed him inside, he asked them to move back against the walls to give him room to dance on the carcass of old Big-Ribs. Up and down on the grass mat he jumped and wheeled, waving his great club and once or twice putting in an

accidental blow. Under the mat Gray Wolf winced
and peered out to choose his meal from among the
onlookers. The fattest one stood furthest from the
door.

"That one!" he yapped, pointing at the fat one.
Wus leaped and caught hold of it by the leg. The
antelopes screamed and scrambled for the door. Wus
was very nearly dragged away by the fellow he held,
but Gray Wolf staggered up and killed it. Much better did he feel after finishing it to the last shred, and
leaning on Wus, he walked out to look at the mountain ridges.

"Almost do I feel as if I might be fast enough to
hunt big game once more. I am eager to taste venison
again, for it is best of all." And then there came to
his mind a plan that seemed a great joke, a plan to
put him in the midst of many deer. Never again
would he have such a chance.

Wus was sent to call the deer. "Come dance! Big-
Ribs is dead! Come dance and we shall throw him
away, toss him out, trample him to dust, be rid of
him forever! Come, Deer! Dance!" And they came.
While the herd danced before the door of the lodge,
Wus and Big Deer carried Gray Wolf out and threw
him to the crowd. But the dead Big-Ribs was very
much alive, a flurry of gray fur and bright teeth.

Deer scattered in all directions, but Gray Wolf was everywhere. Never had he worked so hard, and Wus helped as best he could.

By dusk the lodge was filled with venison enough for weeks, and full were the racks of meat that hung smoking over the fire. Wus was weary and hungry and licked his lips at the thought of a fine supper.

But Gray Wolf drove him away and told him to hunt mice for himself.

The Growing Rock

THE young Bluebird brothers had been praised for their bright clear color, their satin sheen of feather, from the day they had been hatched. They and their mother and father lived at Kowanno, not far from the river, and as chicks they grew to know that neighboring folk spoke well of their bright eyes and fair feathers. Always did they feel, in the days when they were but birdlets, that some bird or other was politely watching them from a branch above or a thicket nearby. Always they walked together, wing to wing, beaks in the air, looking their best.

One morning the two young Bluebird brothers set out to have a swim. Down to the river they went, and in they dipped. The water was fine, the sun shone, and when at last the brothers came out, they searched for a good flat-topped rock where they might stretch out to sun themselves. So warm was the sunshine that soon they fell asleep.

Not long after, while the youngsters slept, Kaai the Crow passed by on his way to draw water from the stream. He frowned. Such a fuss all folk seemed to make over these two spindly fluffs of nothing! There they lay, likely dreaming of fine ornaments and sweet flattery! Most likely they would grow to strut and brag of themselves in the sweathouse, like others of their sort. Tso!

Again he frowned. And then he shut his eyes to wish: "Rock, grow tall. Grow tall to reach the sky. Take those children out of sight. O rock, grow tall and take those children with you!"

The rock seemed to stir, to loosen itself, and then to stretch. Up it went, higher and higher, so smoothly that the brothers slept on. It grew and grew until the sleeping brothers could not be seen. And still it grew. "Stop!" called Crow, but it would not. Crow shrugged, filled his water basket, and set off to his lodge. It was no worry of his, thought he.

Before long, the Bluebirds' mother began to worry. The brothers by now must surely have had their swim. What could have befallen them? She put down her grinding stone and stood up to look around the village. She saw no blue-feathered children. At each lodge she asked, "Has anyone seen my children?"

Everywhere the answer was "No." Crow's door was closed as if no one were at home.

The trail to the river led Old Bluebird past the Growing Rock. "I do not remember such a rock as this before. So tall it is!" She marveled, looking up.

Far above, two heads appeared over its edge, two voices loudly shrieked, "Mother!" but so high were they that it came to her ears as only a whisper.

"My children! My boys!" she wailed. "What shall I do? How came you to be up there?" They heard her not, for the rock still grew, and the world below seemed to sink away more quickly with each passing moment.

Old Bluebird saw that the rock was growing. "What to do? What to do?" she babbled. Someone must help her, for her children did not know how to fly and she herself could not fly so high as that! Back to the village she ran, but there seemed to be no birds around, no strong wings to aid her. To her own lodge she went, and into her largest baskets she poured all of the things of value that she had— beads and belts and shells and porcupine quills and smaller baskets beautifully made. These she carried to the river and set about the base of the Growing

Rock. "Come, my people!" cried she. "Come rescue my chicks, the Bluebird brothers! I offer great rewards. Oh come, my people, and help!"

Quickly the people gathered, for her cries were loud. "All these things," said she to the villagers, pointing to the baskets of fine things, "all these things shall go to the brave who saves my children from this Rock-Which-Grows. Already they are close to the Land-Up-In-The-Sky, and I fear that harm may come to them there. Come, who shall be first to try?"

Buzzard had soared in to join the crowd. "I shall go first," said he, "for I see that no other birds are here. It is good that I am strong. Fear not. I shall rescue your children, good Bluebird."

Off he flew, heavily flapping upward. Higher and higher he climbed, and thirstier and thirstier he grew, until no further than halfway up the height of the rock, he gasped and glided back down. Mountain Lion, whom all knew as a strong climber, was the next to try; but the rock was rough and wore his claws so smooth that he slid backwards down to the ground. He had gone little farther than Buzzard. Mountain Goat and Little Brown Bear and Rock Squirrel tried, and many others after them, but none came near the top.

Frightened, Old Bluebird ran to the village and

sought out the lonely lodge of the last of the menfolk
who were climbers. "O Measuring Worm! Good
Green Measuring Worm! I know that you are aged
and weak, but no one else is left to try the climb.
Please bring my children down to me from the Rock-
Which-Grows! I promise to you many fine gifts of
baskets and ornaments if you will do it."

Measuring Worm creaked out of his bed. "Hai,
so!" He smiled with a toothless grin. "I am old and
stiff to be climbing, but I shall take a look at this
rock of yours and see whether I may try." He took up
his staff and down to the rock they went. Doubtful
he looked when first he saw the Growing Rock. Yet
there was a bit . . . a small piece of a chance. . . .
To do his best, old Measuring Worm hastened back
to his house and made many preparations. To his
head he tied a topknot of feathers. His body he
painted with red paint, and his face he daubed with
black stripes and a smearing of bear grease for
strength. He could feel himself growing stronger.
Quickly he slipped two strands of medicine beads
about his neck, slung his hunting sack across his
back, and made his way once more to the riverbank.

The rock still grew, but Measuring Worm was not
to be dismayed. Up he climbed, humping along,
length by length, foot by foot, on and on, higher and
higher. There were no footholds, no spots to stop to

catch one's breath, and so the old worm moved on steadily. Below, the people saw him creeping higher than had any of the others, and they began to think that he was not such a silly old fellow in his paint and feathers as they had thought at first. Perhaps he *would* bring the Bluebird brothers down!

At its very top, the Growing Rock flared out, much like a mushroom, with an overhanging edge. As Measuring Worm drew near it from below, he paused and hugged the rock tightly with all of his feet. How should he go from here? Never had he made such a climb as this! Backwards—that might be the right way. He would try. Inch by inch, he backed up the last few feet, feeling almost that he hung upside down. At the very edge, he flipped himself head first over onto the top of the rock, almost atop the Bluebird brothers.

The children jumped and shouted with joy. So joyfully did they jump that Measuring Worm feared for their safety and warned them that they might fall. "So high in the sky one must be more than careful," said he. "I will rest, and then we shall see about getting down." In a few moments he drew a deep breath, put the children into his hunting sack, and went back as he had come. The downward trip was not so long, however, for he could slide down easily where he had had to hump his way up so slowly.

Old Bluebird, waiting below, wept happily to see her children, and the whole village cheered old Measuring Worm. They brought water in a basket, washed off his paint, and brought him food and drink. With great cheering they helped him to gather up his reward, to carry his new baskets and shells and ornaments home.

Soon after, Growing Rock began to shrink, and now is as it was at first—but since that day no one has cared to sit upon it.

6552-D-5